TEMPLAT MIXING AND MASTERING

THE ULTIMATE GUIDE TO ACHIEVING A PROFESSIONAL SOUND

TEMPLATE MIXING AND MASTERING

THE ULTIMATE GUIDE TO ACHIEVING A PROFESSIONAL SOUND

BILLY DECKER AND **SIMON TAYLOR**

FOREWORD BY RODNEY ATKINS

The Crowood Press

First published in 2020 by
The Crowood Press Ltd
Ramsbury, Marlborough
Wiltshire SN8 2HR

enquiries@crowood.com

This impression 2021

www.crowood.com

British Library Cataloguing-in-Publication Data
A catalogue record for this book is available from the British Library.

ISBN 978 1 78500 749 1

Foreword image: Courtesy of Rodney Atkins.

Typeset by Jean Cussons Typesetting, Diss, Norfolk
Printed and bound in India by Parksons Graphics Pvt. Ltd., Mumbai.

CONTENTS

Foreword by Rodney Atkins   7

Introduction   9

1   Building your Template   17

2   Drums   25

3   Instruments   45

4   Vocals   57

5   The Master Channel   67

6   Importing Audio and Gain Staging   71

7   Mixing   77

8   Mastering   93

9   Other Considerations   99

In Closing   107

About Billy Decker   109

Appendix A – Mixing Desk Channels   111

Appendix B – Plugin Effects and Processors   112

Glossary   115

Index   127

FOREWORD

I like to think of myself as a Shade Tree Song Mechanic. When making records, I believe one quarter of the process is in the writing, one quarter is in the recording and half is in the mixing. The art of mixing is that you can take a song to another level or completely lose it. Billy Decker is an innovator, a NASCAR Song Mechanic, fearless and undaunted by anything I can dream up. He hears what isn't there and then makes it appear. He is the secret to my success. I have tried to work with other mix engineers, but came to the realization that no one can achieve sounds that even come close to the ones Decker creates. He is truly an artist. His canvas is silence. He fills it with colours, feelings and emotions that move people, whilst simplifying everything he does. His comprehension of his tools is beyond compare, and this book is a gift of gratitude to anyone that wants to stop trying to fit in to the landscape of records that sound the same and take a step into out-of-this-world-sounding songs. I encourage you to take your time reading this book, practise what he preaches and listen for all the pieces to fall into place.

Rodney Atkins

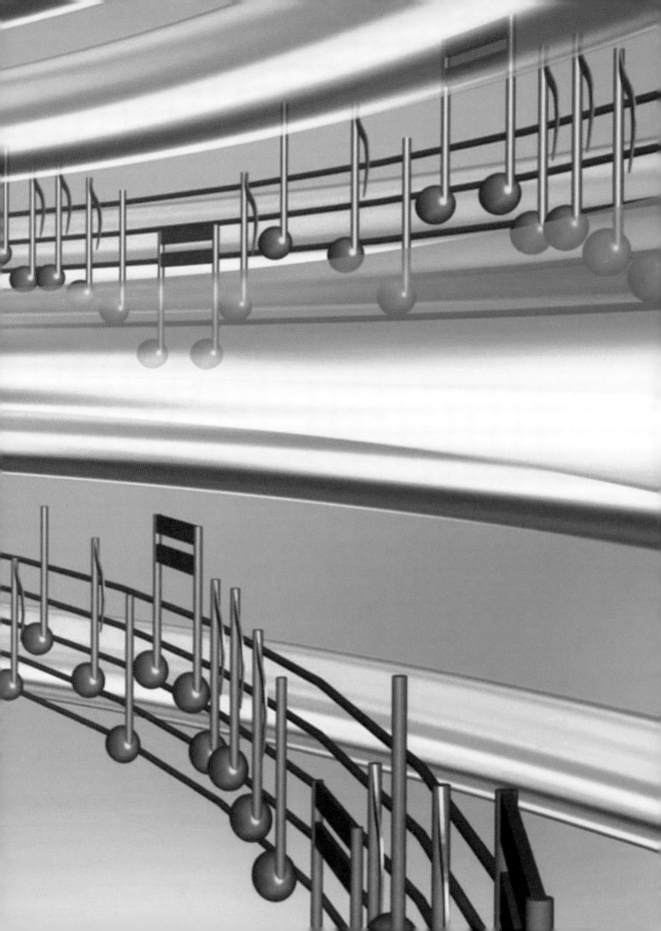

INTRODUCTION

Music is undeniably one of humankind's greatest achievements. It is an art form that manifests in each and every one of us. From the moment we are born we create sound. We marvel at the beauty of the melodies, rhythms and harmonies that play out the soundtrack to our lives. It is these musical wonders that we mix engineers must portray in their finest glory by sculpting what we refer to as 'a mix'. There are many ways of achieving a great mix. Each individual engineer will have their own methods of production that make up his or her sound. I'd like to tell you my way in the hope that it will help you in your quest to be the best you can be.

Where are you on your musical journey? Are you just starting out and discouraged from taking your first step because you don't know how? Thinking it will take too long to learn? You won't be good enough? Maybe you have been mixing for a while and are struggling to improve? Wondering how 'pro' mixers mix? What are they doing that I am not? How do they mix so many songs in the time I struggle to finish one? Why am I making the same mistakes on each mix and not progressing as a mixer? You may already be proficient at mixing and simply want to know how I work.

Whether you are a complete novice, an emerging talent, or a practising music professional, this book will walk you through each step of your new mixing journey. I will share with you the secrets of my methodology. It has evolved over twenty years of my mistake-making and experimentation, which I have now honed into a super-fast machine. How do I do it? Well the good news is I only use a standard computer with software that is available to anyone. I use a 'mix template' on every mix I do, the same mix template that is contained within these pages and which has blessed me with my success.

As we work through this book together, each chapter will provide you with straightforward instructions, tips and tricks. You will learn what a mix template is, how to create one, and how to optimize your audio. I will show you how to use effects and processors the 'Deckerator' way as we progress your mix through to completion, finishing with a method of mastering you can perform at your own workstation. You will see from my workflow that I make life as simple as possible in my approach. That's how I can mix really fast. Most of my mixes are sent to the client after around forty-five minutes to an hour's work. Instead of spending two hours equalizing a kick drum, I can do it in thirty seconds. I then focus on the things that really matter like fine-tuning, bringing levels up and down, and working on the entire mix.

Music production has never been so exciting. There has never been such an array of tools with which to shape sound. However, I have found that what creates a successful mix is a template that you know inside out. One that contains a few well-chosen plugins that remain constant for every mix you do. My vocal channel effects chain hasn't changed for the last ten years! I will show you what it takes to get your template rocking. You will learn how to play your DAW (digital audio workstation) like an instrument and coax the very best out of it. Soon, with your passion, patience and practice you too will be mixing quickly and professionally.

WHAT IS 'THE DECKER WAY'?

Well, what it is not is a rewrite of the standard book for mixing. It was never my intention to repeat what has already been written many times before. What you will find is the buried treasure that you could spend literally years trying to discover elsewhere: the gold nuggets of information that really make a difference.

'The Decker way' is a complete system for mixing and mastering. It shows you how to set up and mix multi-track recordings on a digital audio workstation to a professional level. It's easy to find many partial bits of informa-tion here, there and everywhere, from industry online forums,

Any standard computer can be used to mix multi-track recordings, and there is a wide range of top-quality free software available to get you started.

physical books and e-books on the internet. What this will give you is absolutely every setting from each individual channel strip, complete with plugin suggestions and parameters to input. This could be all you'll ever need. It is all I ever use. Whether you choose to embellish this set-up is up to you, but this system is built on a streamlined workflow with speed and elegance that's hard to beat – there are also a few surprising twists along the way.

This way of mixing is for anyone who owns a computer and mixes multi-track recordings.

This is the very same system that I use every day on every mix I do, and will literally save you years of searching for the same answers that I did. It comprises the following:

1. Detailed instructions on how to build your template complete with all routing, plugins and channel settings.
2. Information on how to import audio into your template and optimize it using my method of gain staging.

3. An insight into how I mix and the methods I employ, including my good practice and work-flow suggestions.
4. My mastering processor chain. Your mixes can now be mastered within the mix session should you so choose.

WHY A TEMPLATE?

Once I'd made the decision to focus entirely on mixing, I knew I had to find a workflow that allowed me to be home in time for dinner! I remember my wife and kids not being happy because I was away all the time at the studio. I was missing my son and daughter growing up and quality time with my family. I was tired of having to spend hours recalling the mixing console and setting up all the outboard gear. Then someone showed me Pro Tools and I thought, 'Wow, I'm gonna mix on this thing'. I could instantly see the potential for super-fast set-up times and the total recall possibilities that would enable me to roll from one song to another. This in turn led to the discovery of templates. A set-up that used to take me an hour or so in the analogue world now took just a minute to load a template.

You may already know about templates, and be reading this and thinking, 'I don't have time to set up a template' or 'I could be mixing when all I'm doing is setting up tracks, routing and plugins'. Well, yes, you could, and setting up a template does take time – expect to set aside a day to complete the task. But don't underestimate the knowledge you will gain from going through this process. You will get to know your template inside out, which will in turn allow you to play your DAW like an instrument with skill and professional expertise. You may be thinking, 'Just give us your template!' Yes I could give you a copy of my template, but you would spend more time scratching your head trying to work out what was going on than you will setting it up from scratch. This way you are empowered to own it completely. When your template is finished it is yours for life, mix after mix after mix. Set up once and use forever.

I once mixed seventeen songs in one day! Imagine how long it would have taken me to initiate all the routing, plugins and channel settings for just one of those songs.

When you have your template set up you will simply import the audio files, apply my gain-staging method and press play. You will find that you are already very close to your final mix within minutes. You are then free to focus on the overall mix. A fine-tuning of EQ settings and subtle balancing between instruments is all that's required.

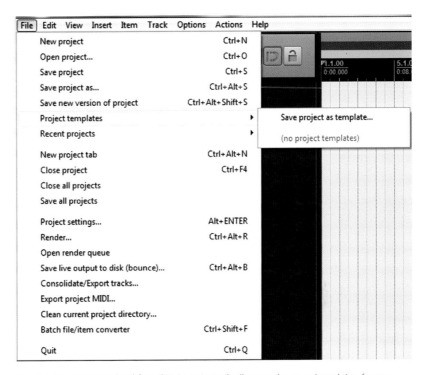

Use the 'save as template' function to automatically organize your templates for you.

WHAT IS A TEMPLATE?

To know a template you need to know a DAW. If you are reading this book then you probably already own a DAW or you are thinking of getting one. A DAW is a piece of software that runs on a personal computer. It allows musicians to capture sound via a soundcard, which is then represented as a waveform image along a timeline. A DAW usually, but not always, has two work areas; the tracking section (commonly called the 'editor') and the mixer section. The tracking/editor screen is where recorded sound appears and is edited against time; the mixer section is where the musical elements are combined. It is basically a digital representation of the old analogue tape recorder and mixing desk scenario. But the computer is capable of remembering absolutely every parameter you can think of. This is called 'total recall' – the ability to recall your entire song. Everything from audio tracks, mixing-desk settings, automation and so much more is recalled in an instant, and we manage all this information within one compact file called a template.

You may have been using a DAW for many years but have never used a template, instead choosing to set up everything from scratch each time you mix. Take a moment to think of all the time you spend doing the same repetitive tasks and actions that could and should be automated – welcome to the world of templates.

WHICH DAW

In order to build your mix template you will need a DAW. Which DAW you choose is entirely up to you. In simplistic terms, no DAW is any better than another. They essentially all do the same thing. One DAW may offer more features than another, or target a specific area of audio production, but the best DAW for any one person is a DAW they know inside out, a DAW on which they can perform any task without the need to think.

Your goal should be to learn to play your DAW like an instrument and become part of it. This means reading your DAW manual from front to back, then back to front again. It means learning all the shortcut keys that give the user speed and a professional flow. Practise the moves you perform the most so that the mouse, keyboard and VDU become part of you and not something external. You will soon forget you are even doing it and never again have to think about which keys to press as second nature takes over.

While you are learning these skills refer only to your manual as it contains all you need. Internet searches and online forums will severely interrupt your focus, so limit these to your fun time when you are not mixing. Do your research, choose your DAW and stick with it forevermore. Don't fall into the trap of thinking a better DAW will give you better mixes – it won't. You will simply lose many hours of valuable mixing time. I use Avid Pro Tools, but I could easily be using any other DAW, it really doesn't matter.

The information contained within this book can be applied to any DAW. You will get great results and sound through the decisions you take, not the specification or any one tool. There is no single magic bullet for mixing.

FUNDAMENTAL REQUIREMENTS AND CONVENTIONS

If all of this is new to you, please do not be discouraged by the technical content. Setting up your template can be as easy as copying the parameters I have logged, importing your audio, pressing play, listening and adapting by instinct – no advanced knowledge is needed. The only basic requirements that you will need are: to have made your choice of DAW, read its manual and formed a basic foundation of knowledge regarding the following:

1. Opening and saving session files
2. Saving your session in a template format
3. Adding and managing tracks and channels
4. Adding effects and processors (plugins)
5. Importing and exporting audio
6. Routing channel inputs and outputs from source to destination

I am aware that the technical words we use can have different meanings to different people in the industry, so the convention I am using is this:

- A 'track' refers to a single area running horizontally within the timeline of the editor/tracking screen. Audio is recorded, or imported to a track.
- A 'channel' refers to a single vertical channel strip within the mixing screen. Audio is passed through a channel.
- A 'buss' is a destination to which one or more sound sources can be routed and controlled as one. Think of this as a submix of everything routed to it.
- The 'master channel' is the stereo channel to which all other channels are routed.

- Effects and processors will be referred to as 'plugins', a plugin being the universally recognized name describing both digital effects and processors.

I discourage unnecessary, time-consuming tasks such as colouring tracks for specific instrument groups, inputting section markers, renaming tracks or the use of complicated buss routing. If your DAW creates random colours by default then leave it be; there is no need to spend time "uncolouring" them. Simplicity is the key here; I have even learned how to minimize riding faders too! This method uses a lot of very light compression and limiting; the plugins do the work for you, so as to cut out the unnecessary, time-consuming things that seem small on their own but add up. This will get you into the habit of importing your audio into the template, then going straight into mixing.

The best way to understand the flexibility and power of this template is to follow the instructions exactly. This will give you the best foundation to go on and you can customize it in your own way as you have fun tweaking, playing, practising, and making it your own over time. Think of this as the starting point on your journey on the pathway that leads to pro mixes FAST!

I will be showing you parameters for each of your channel strip's components in the order they appear on most conventional mixing consoles: input followed by insert effects, auxiliary send and returns, panning, fader and output.

Please name each channel and enter each parameter given exactly as described. This will make it easier for you to understand the interaction that goes on between all parts of the template. Only by doing this will you hear what I am

hearing and think what I am thinking. You can customize the template and make it your own when you've finished setting up and you are totally familiar with how it works.

It is assumed that all effects and processors will be inserted pre-fader. If you are unsure about the differences between pre- and post-sends, inserts, aux sends, or whether a plugin is an effect or a processor, then now is the time to consult your DAW manual. It has all the answers and is much less of a distraction than searching on the internet. It is not the intent of this book to educate you in all areas of music technology, but rather to show you how to optimize the DAW you have before you turn into a streamlined hit-making machine.

As we learned earlier, a template is the sum of all the parts of a DAW. This includes the virtual mixing desk, effects processors, source audio, track layouts, visual settings and user preferences to name a few. The list goes on and on, but most parameters are set automatically when you open a new session and are saved when you close it. So

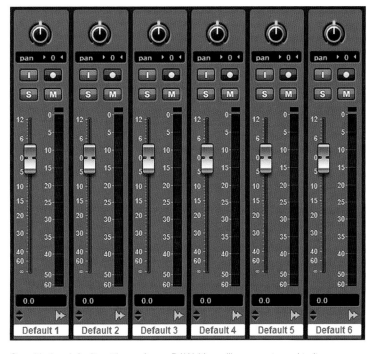

Go with the default settings of your DAW. You will soon get used to its idiosyncrasies.

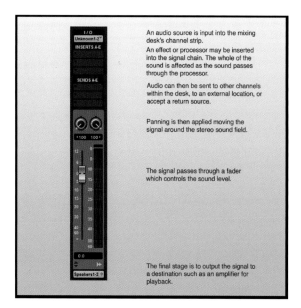

A basic knowledge of how an audio signal flows through a mixing desk is all that is needed to start routing audio through your template.

in reality there are only a few we need to concern ourselves with. We'll cover them all in the following chapters starting with our biggest concern, the mixing desk, complete with all its effects and processors. We'll walk through each step one at a time, channel by channel, in the very same way that my virtual mixing desk is laid out.

Should you wish to sneak a quick peak at the template as a whole you can jump to the back of the book where you will find a full list of channels in Appendix A and all the plugins in their glory within Appendix B. Over time, you will be tempted by all the latest products that are marketed with all the usual bells and whistles to supposedly change your life. The reality is that there is no magic bullet; there is no one tool that can do the mixing for you. I rarely even upgrade the tools I have, and then only when it is absolutely necessary that I do for the continued working of my template.

I have always said, 'I get paid to practise every day!' From day one, I wanted to get better and the only way you can get better is to practise. The great thing about living in Nashville is that there is always going to be a song to mix; but you too can

always find songs to practise on. Just ask around or make friends on the internet – you'll be amazed at the response.

But, of course, there are many ways to mix a multi-track recording and what I am about to show you is my unique way. Hopefully you will take it and run with it and never look back. But even if you find the complete Deckerator experience is not for you, I am confident that parts of this book will stay with you for life and find their way into your daily workflow regardless.

PLUGIN EFFECTS AND PROCESSORS

A quick word about plugins; I have purposely not named my plugins in the main text because I wanted to make it clear that you can mix to a professional standard with whatever tools you have to hand. Brand names and today's flavour of the month will come and go but a compressor will always be a compressor. You may have heard the saying 'It's in the ear, not the gear'. I have always found this to be true. Whenever someone says to me, 'What's your favourite piece of gear?' or 'What gear couldn't you mix without?' I always point to my ears!

So, whatever you have at your disposal, whether it's a £40/$50 DAW with stock plugins or a £1,500/$2,000 DAW loaded with all the pro packages known to man, remember this: if one of the many A-list mix engineers walked into your studio today to mix that very song you are mixing right now, on the same system you are using, within a few hours he or she would have a great-sounding pro mix banging out of your speakers, without a doubt. Why? Because they know where they are going before they start. They will have a clear picture in their mind that has been sculpted over years of listening to music and practising mixing. They each have a unique visual landscape that is their destination, and no matter what stands in their way they know how to get there through experience and hard work, not because of the latest fad.

We will talk about this later in more detail but the point to take away here is this: use whatever you have at your disposal and don't look for excuses; whatever you have is more than enough.

Having said that, all plugins sound and react differently to each other. There are good and bad plugins, the same as there are good and bad musicians, guitars, singers, etc. You are about to audition and choose your own favourite go-to effects and processors from your available arsenal, plugins that will form the basis of your template. So what should you look for? Well, sound obviously, but almost as important is being able to navigate through a plugin quickly and easily.

I would like to state that I am in no way endorsing any of the plugins I use. I have included a list of my template plugins in Appendix B at the back of the book, as I feel that the book would be incomplete without this information, but it is up to you to choose which manufacturer's plugin you include in your template. The brand of plugin is not as important as you may think. The important point is to use the same type of plugin so you gain the same control over the audio firing its way through your template.

Having said that, most of the makers of the plugins I use offer a free 'try before you buy' period, so it could be an interesting exercise to download a trial of the plugins I use and try to match them with the ones you have at your disposal. There are many wonderful free plugins available today both as stock plugins within your DAW and made by other third-party providers.

I am including the input and output stages of all my plugins for completeness but in reality yours will probably be different unless you have the exact same plugin as me. Just tweak as is needed to optimize the signal flow and get the very best out of each processor.

A quick word on analogue modelling within plugins: many plugins have an analogue function that creates the noise of the original circuitry and can be switched in or out. Please turn these off. This is a crazy idea in my opinion. I've spent years trying to get away from noise and lessen

My old Avid Pro Control desk is one example of a mixing desk.

its impact; the last thing I want to do is add it back in!

And finally, insert mono plugins on mono channels and stereo plugins on stereo channels.

THE MIXING DESK

The mixing desk has always been central to a recording studio. Whenever you see a photograph of a famous mix engineer or a recording session of your favourite band they will be pictured alongside a huge mixing desk. This continues to be the case in the modern digital world. The mixing console is still central to our musical endeavours, albeit in a virtual form. Every single musical note that is voiced must pass through a virtual or real-world mixing desk at some stage on its journey. The mixing desk is where all things are combined into the stereo sound-field image that is our musical canvas.

I still own an Avid Pro Control desk, but it acts only as a volume control for the monitors these days. I keep it as it impresses customers; it looks good in photographs and gives me the feel of mixing behind a desk, but I mix 100 per cent in-the-box. Even if you don't possess a physical mixing desk, it helps to envision your DAW as this type of device.

1
BUILDING YOUR TEMPLATE

The template covered in the following chapters is an exact copy of my template that I have used to mix no. 1 Billboard hit records, and the very same template I use every day on every mix I do. It contains all the common elements found in popular music and can be used to mix anything from pop to metal.

When starting a template for the first time, it is essential that you create a new blank session within your DAW without any previous routing or settings that may confuse the process. We will work our template from left to right in the actual order the channels appear on my DAW, starting with the drums and then progressing through the instruments to end with the vocals.

It is important to realize that what we are about to create is designed to get you straight into the ballpark within moments. That does not mean that you won't need to make minor alterations to certain plugin levels and settings. This will be most apparent the first time you use your template. Unless you have the exact same plugins and DAW as me some minor adjustments will be inevitable, so be prepared. From the first mix onwards though, you will quickly iron out any initial teething problems, trust me. Your current best mix will be your go-to template. Simply save it as your master template to use forevermore.

As mentioned previously, our adventure begins with the drum section before walking through the instruments, vocals and master channels one by one, so let us start our preparation for the drum section.

I am known in Nashville as 'the vocal guy' but would love to be known as 'the drum guy'. My drum sound is big, open and bright with a radio-friendly vibe, which I achieve by combining real drums with samples.

Don't underestimate the power drums have over your mix. Drums are life. Bass drums sell songs and the drum section, with its thirty-six plugins and twenty-two channels, represents nearly half of our entire template, such is its importance.

I'd like to prime you with a brief overview showing how I set up and utilize my complete drum section. This will hopefully help you prepare for the task ahead.

The process is this: I take a few carefully chosen samples and either replace or blend them with the real sounds. Without exception I always totally replace the bass-drum part I am given with three different samples. None of the real bass-drum sound remains. The original source audio is kept only to trigger the samples, thus retaining the human dynamic. For the snare drum and the tom toms the real sounds are blended with samples. No EQ is needed (except for a one-off 'set and leave' EQ) and very few instances of reverb exist, one of which is a snare reverb sample triggered by the snare drum. I use two channels of parallel compression – one on the snare samples and one on the bass, snare and tom-tom submix. These are then combined back with the original dry sounds via the main drum buss, which is then treated once more to a subtle layer of multiple processing. I send the overheads, room microphones and hi-hats straight to the master buss, bypassing the drum buss and any parallel compression.

If the above doesn't make much sense to you, don't worry, it will all be broken down and explained as we progress. At least you now have a vision of where you are going – even if it's a bit blurred!

For the kick and snare drums we will place three different samples across three mixer channels and for the tom toms we will collate our three samples in one 'drum replacer' plugin. We can then quickly blend these, as if we were using them as tone controls, to find the right balance for the mix. This is the best way I have found to get maximum flexibility, speed of use and, of course, a great sound.

DRUM REPLACEMENT TECHNOLOGY

Within the final paragraphs of preparation I would like to discuss drum replacement technology, the drum samples I use and what to look out for when you select your samples.

Drum replacement technology is the act of replacing or blending real sounds with samples. I believe this is a major part of achieving a contemporary drum sound. Using samples to replace, or blend with, the drum hits a drummer plays is a fantastic way of controlling the quality and consistency of the drums in every mix you do, and consistency of a certain level equals professionalism.

I always use drum replacement technology in every mix I do and have done so for as long as I can remember. I use the same kick, snare, toms and snare reverb samples just about every time – I just blend them differently for varying textures and sounds. So to maximize the potential of your template I recommend you employ samples too.

You can do one of two things to replace real drums with samples. You can do as I do and use a plugin to handle the process or place the samples by hand along the timeline of the song.

If you are new to the concept of sample replacement, it goes like this. The captured audio of a real drummer's performance is fed through a drum replacer plugin. Every time the real drummer hits, for example, a snare drum, the drum replacer triggers a sample loaded into the interface. Whether the sample totally replaces the real hit or blends with it is up to you and the settings you apply. Additional parameters allow control over the other features, for example the ADSR envelope and the threshold on which the sample triggers.

This is an easy and convenient way of handling the task. However, don't feel you need a plugin at all. Many engineers still place their samples by hand. They feel it gives them ultimate control over how a sample sounds. When placing by hand there is no doubt over what the sample is doing, when it starts and ends and how long it plays for, it is all there for the eye to see and the ears to hear. Leaving the task to a piece of software can be a leap of faith and needs knowledge

You can place drum samples by hand if a drum replacer is not in your kitbag.

of how the plugin works to avoid missing beats or samples triggering when they shouldn't! So just because you don't have access to a drum replacer don't feel this is something you are excluded from. Many top engineers still choose to place samples by hand and you can too.

DRUM SAMPLES

Our first exercise here is to think about the sound qualities of individual samples and how they blend together. I will show you how I build my sound and then you can choose to match it or go your own way. Much will depend on your musical style and preference. You can then go and find your samples in preparation for importing them into your template. Here is a list of the samples I use and their musical qualities.

KICK DRUM
1. J-KIK: Accentuates the click of the kick drum.

It is worth noting that at no point will I add any reverberation to my kick drum samples. I aim for a dry, upfront sound.

2. D-KIK: Brings a low mid thump to the mix.

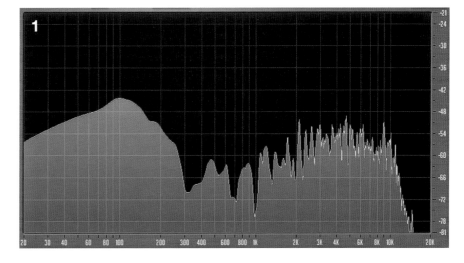

The sample I use for the J-KIK channel has an accentuated 'clicky' sound.

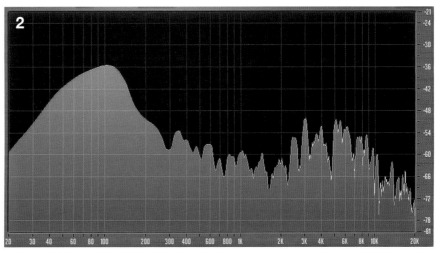

The D-KIK sounds very much like a dance music kick drum.

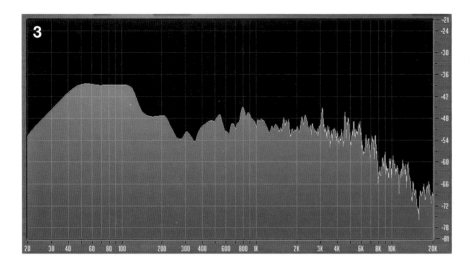

The final H-KIK sample provides the 'whoosh' or 'push' sound that I like to add to the kick drum blend.

3. H-KIK: Gives me the 'whoosh' or 'push' sound I like.

All three samples have contrasting tones, each bringing something unique to the combined kick sound.

SNARE DRUM

1. FATTY: Represents the low-end weight of the snare.

Many engineers will load up three or four samples in one drum replacer and treat the whole blend with compressors and EQ. I like to keep my samples separate to make the whole process more versatile.

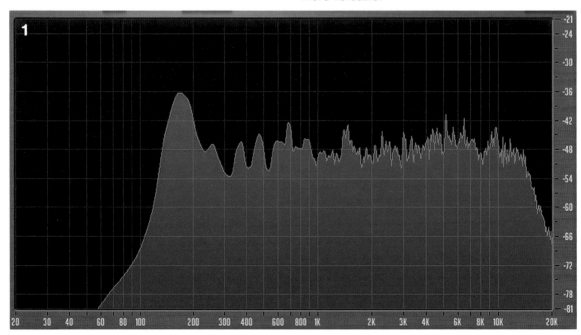

There is plenty of low-end weight in the FATTY sample I use and I am going to emphasize that low end further with EQ in my channel strip.

With my MID snare sample I am highlighting the mid area of the frequency spectrum.

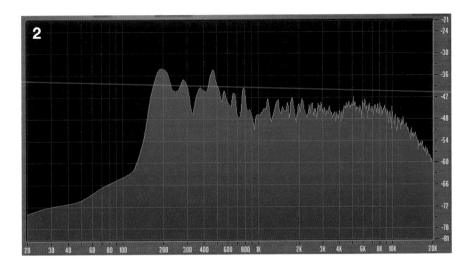

I use a sample with an extended top end to represent the HIGH frequencies of my snare submix.

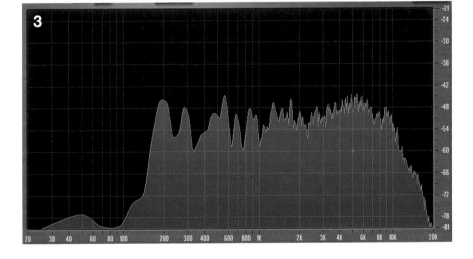

2. MID: Gives an accentuated mid range when blended.

Keep in mind it is not how the samples sound in isolation that counts, but how they blend as one.

3. HIGH: Adds the 'crack' or 'snap'.

All three of these snare samples contain very little ambience. I have kept the room sound to a minimum as I will be adding controlled reverb by way of a triggered snare reverberation sample on a separate channel.

SNARE REVERB

Added to my combined snare sound is a classic snare reverb sample with the top and bottom rolled off to add just the right amount of reverb every time, hit after hit.

TOM 1

Three individual samples for a classic high tom sound.

For this and each of my tom channels I actually use a blend of three samples within one instance of a drum replacer. The diagrams you see here

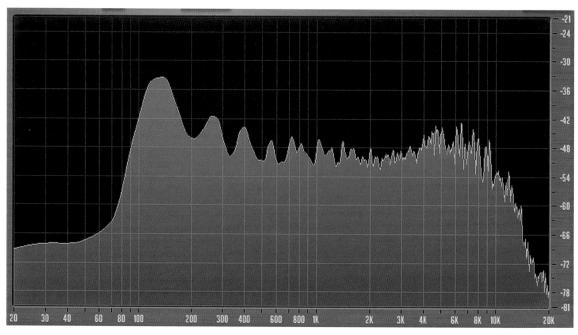

TOM 1: The highest sounding Tom.

show the output of each drum replacer (i.e. a combined output of the three samples). Use one sample or multiple samples, it matters not. Shoot for your favourite tone. If it sounds good, it is good.

TOM 2
A blend of samples to make my second tom sound.

I am aiming for a classic tom sound, which I will then shape with an EQ plugin.

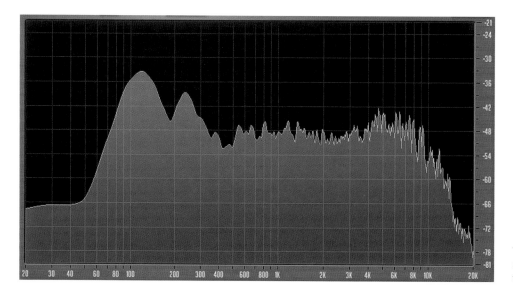

TOM 2: The middle of the three Toms.

Tom 3

As before, three samples create a low tom sub-mix.

I am blonding three samples again and measuring the combined output of the channel. What you are seeing in all these frequency curves is the pure drum sound without any additional EQ and compression applied. Also, as previously stated, there will be no additional reverberation added to the drum channels, so if you want a 'roomy' sound add it into your chosen samples.

My kick, snare and toms are each made up of a blend of three samples. As you look for your own signature sounds, think of each individual sample as representing three musical attributes of the whole sound as in my kick drum, i.e. click, mid punch and whoosh, or three areas of the frequency spectrum – low, mid and high.

Using samples will enable you to achieve consistent, repeatable and reliable results. I know that with my trusty samples I can get the same sound always, no matter how good or poor the quality of the recordings I am given.

Whatever your tastes and however you gather your samples (stock hits, sample libraries, free internet sounds, banging wooden spoons on your fridge door!) go find your personality, your hits, your sound and save them in a folder ready for the next chapter. This is going to have a big impact on your mixes. Have fun with it and take your time auditioning each sample and testing how well samples blend together. Each sample should have its own unique sound, totally unlike any other. You can always revisit your samples and improve your combinations as your sound progresses.

So, moving forward, open, name and save a blank session. Now with the session open let's begin constructing our hit-making template.

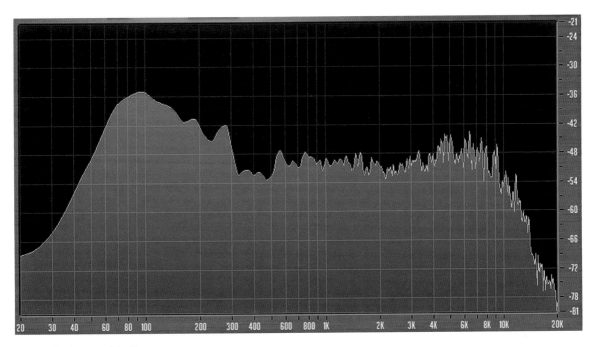

TOM 3: The lowest of the Toms.

2
DRUMS

THE DRUM SECTION

CHANNEL 1: KICK DRUM SAMPLE A

Insert the first new track/channel in your blank template and name it 'J-KIK'. All tracks are 'Mono' unless stated otherwise. When you add a new track to a project it appears as a new addition to the 'edit' window. This automatically creates a corresponding mixer strip channel in the 'mix' window. You can't have one without the other, unless you are using a single-screen DAW with no separate 'mix' window.

Just go with me on these channel names – you can rename them later when you are familiar with their function. In the first feature box is the first mixer channel in the format that all subsequent channels will follow. The first heading named 'Insert Fx' lists the plugins I want you to insert; then follows the 'Sends and Returns', 'Panning', 'Fader' and 'Output' for you to enter. Please copy each channel exactly into your DAW, including the fader and panning levels. Routing of all sends and returns is covered later once all channels have been created. Finally, in the second feature

The majority of DAWs have two main areas to work in; the edit and mix windows.

box, the 'Plugins Expanded' dialogue contains a detailed list of the parameters found within each plugin; this is where I talk you through the purpose of each plugin and how I use it.

Insert Fx

1. Drum replacer
2. Channel strip

Sends and Returns

N/a

Panning

Centre

Fader

−3.5db

Output

Master

Plugins Expanded

1. Drum replacer

Mix	100 per cent wet
Decay	Short

The first plugin that appears on our template is a drum replacement plugin. This will trigger your first drum sample (as discussed previously), so now is the time to insert your plugin, locate and load your carefully chosen sample and you're good to go.

Each make of drum replacer will have different controls to shape the envelope of the drum sound and blend the sample with the real sound. You can have a play with these once we've set up, but there are only two parameters that we should concern ourselves with at this stage and those are: 1. the decay – most samples will benefit from a reduced decay setting so always look to trim this to taste; 2. we want to hear the sample only, none of the original sound, so set the mix dial to 100 per

cent wet. The first of my three kick samples has a 'click' element to it.

If you have chosen to place your samples by hand, just ignore all the occurrences of drum replacers. It's still important to have control over the envelope of the sound though. You can easily shape the decay of your sample by manipulating the end and fade handle of the clip.

2. Channel strip

Filter	
HPF	70Hz

Equalizer			
+6db	62Hz	Bell shape	Medium Q
−12db	250Hz	Bell shape	Medium Q – wide Q
+4db	1.5kHz	Bell shape	Medium Q
+6db	8kHz	Bell shape	Medium Q

Compressor	
Threshold	−20
Release	Fast
Ratio	3:1
Attack	Slow

Our second plugin is a channel strip emulation (not to be confused with the main J-KIK mixer channel strip). We are using the filter, EQ and compressor sections. There are a few interesting points to note here; notice how the filter is set higher than the lowest boosting EQ band. A filter is an attenuating sloping curve that reduces additional frequencies other than the point of reference – so it's actually cutting the boost! By moving the filter beyond a frequency boost we can soften the impact. To me it just sounds better this way. Also, the upper mid boost is fun and is what defines the 'clickiness'. Try boosting this band by +6db and moving between 2kHz, 5kHz and then 8kHz to get a variety of clicks; you can almost change the whole sound just on this one band.

Moving on to the compressor; set the ratio to 3:1 with a slow attack to let the majority of the body of the sound through. The higher the threshold the smaller the sound, so light compression with a slow attack lets the majority of the fullness be heard.

CHANNEL 2: KICK DRUM SAMPLE B

Insert a new track/channel and name it 'D-KIK'.

Insert Fx

3. Drum replacer

Sends and Returns

N/a

Panning

Centre

Fader

–7.4db

Output

Master

Plugins Expanded

3. Drum replacer

Mix	100 per cent wet
Decay	Short

Plugin no. 3 is quite straightforward. If you are using a drum replacer, insert it now and load your sample. Just be sure to set the mix to 100 per cent wet and keep the decay short as per the previous channel.

The sample I use adds the low-mid punch, which sounds to me like a dance music kick drum or a basketball thud. Your sample should do the same, i.e. enhance the low mids.

CHANNEL 3: KICK DRUM SAMPLE C

Insert a new track/channel and name it 'H-KIK'.

Insert Fx

4. Drum replacer

Sends and Returns

N/a

Panning

Centre

Fader

–3.5db

Output

Master

Plugins Expanded

4. Drum replacer

Mix	100 per cent wet
Decay	Short

Plugin no. 4 is once more the drum replacer. This is the third and final kick drum sample that we will blend with the previous two to form one diverse and interesting kick drum sound. The sample I use adds what I refer to as the whoosh or push sound that I like to hear in the kick drum blend. Keep the mix 100 per cent wet at all times and make the decay short to control the overhang of the samples.

A quick recap shows that we now have three samples (A, B and C) all of which will be triggered by the real performance of the live drummer or placed by hand within the mix timeline. Either way they will fully replace the original kick drum. We now have clicky, low mid and push samples that all blend to one kick drum sound.

CHANNEL 4: REVERSE CYMBAL

Insert a new stereo track/channel and name it 'Cym Rev'.

Insert Fx

5. Equalizer

Sends and Returns

N/a

Panning

Centre

Fader

+2.4db

Output

Master

Plugins Expanded

5. Equalizer

+5.5db	13.8kHz	Bell shape	Medium Q

This track/channel is for any reverse cymbal or reverse sound that builds prior to the chorus. You know the trick; you will have heard it many times. You might think a reverse cymbal is a strange choice to follow the bass drums; the reason I like it here is so that I can lock the end of the cymbal to a bass-drum hit. Placing a reverse cymbal track next to a kick drum is the perfect way to ensure that the timing is spot on and that the cymbal cuts out the moment the bass drum kicks in.

There is one parametric EQ on this channel adding some air.

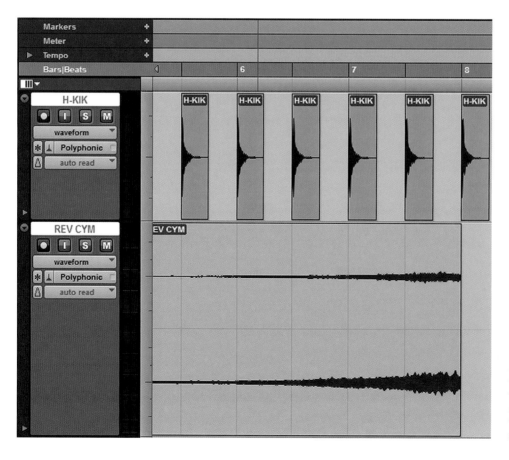

Most modern productions have a reverse cymbal or similar effect that adds tension as the music builds towards a section change.

CHANNEL 5: SNARE TOP

Insert a new track/channel and name it 'SNR Top'.

Insert Fx
6. Channel strip
7. Clipper

Sends and Returns
N/a

Panning
Centre

Fader
−6.4db

Output
Master

Plugins Expanded
6. Channel strip

HPF	170Hz
LPF	5kHz

Equalizer			
+6db	700Hz	Bell shape	Narrow – medium Q
+6db	8kHz	Shelf	

Compressor	
Threshold	−15
Attack	Fast
Release	Fast
Ratio	3:1
Attenuation	3db max

This channel contains the actual audio as played by the drummer and captured by the microphone positioned above the snare drum and pointing down at the top snare skin.

A microphone recording the top skin of a snare drum.
Created from images by Blubberfisch, Pixabay and Tonischerrenberg, Pixabay.

If you are mixing a track that has been pro-grammed into a drum synthesizer using MIDI, export the performance to audio and treat it as though it came from the sticks of your favourite rhythmic maestro.

The first plugin to insert is channel strip emula-tion. We are using the filters, EQ and compressor stages. With the filters and EQ we're filtering out the trash and adding some weight and presence. See the production trick where the filter is lower than the boost. I don't know why that works but it does. The filter clips off all the frequencies above 5kHz and then the shelving boost brings up the top just a little, for some overall brightness. By overlapping the frequencies, you can achieve a softer brightness.

Regarding the compression stage, you'll notice that I have set a fast attack for this one. A fast attack is great for adding that snap to your snare, but only compress it about 2–3db max, any more than that and the sound disappears and you negate what you're trying to do, so keep it light.

Plugins Expanded
7. Clipper

25 per cent (3 lights)

Plugin no. 7 is our first look at a 'clipper'. Any plugin that calls itself a clipper will do. A good peak clipper will preserve the transients and add to the boldness of the source, making it louder without increasing actual gain. It works by care-

fully reducing momentary peaks in a manner that won't affect the overall quality, and it also has a cleaner sound with fewer side effects than a brick-wall limiter, for example.

For me, this just gives a touch more presence by making the snare drum louder without changing the sound. Whichever clipper you choose, look to increase the power of the source by around 25 per cent – on my choice of plugin that's three lights.

CHANNEL 6: SNARE BOTTOM

Insert a new track/channel and name it 'SNR Bot'.

Insert Fx

8. Channel strip

Sends and Returns

N/a

Panning

Centre

Fader

–13.7

Output

Master

Plugins Expanded
8. Channel strip

Filter	
HPF	300Hz
LPF	9kHz

Equalizer			
+6db	700Hz	Bell shape	Narrow – medium Q
+6db	8kHz	Shelf	

Compressor	
Threshold	–20
Attack	Slow
Release	Fast
Ratio	3:1
Attenuation	3db max

Your snare bottom channel is where you will place the real snare-drum recording that has been captured by the microphone positioned below the snare drum and pointing up at the bottom snare skin.

There is not a whole lot going on. I blend in just a bit of this channel sometimes. Often I won't use it at all. The only time it is really of use is when the drummer plays with brushes and you want the sound of the metal snares to come through.

All the channel strip is doing is rolling off the trash top and bottom and adding some weight and presence with 2–3db compression at most. Gentle, multiple layers of compression and limiting throughout the template give controlled profes-sional results.

A microphone recording the bottom skin of a snare drum. *Created from images by Blubberfisch, Pixabay and Tonischerrenberg, Pixabay.*

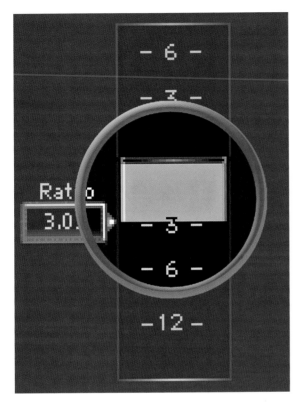

2-3 decibels of gain reduction is all that is needed from our army of dynamic processors.

CHANNEL 7: SNARE SAMPLE A

Insert a new track/channel and name it 'Fatty'.

Insert Fx

9. Drum replacer

10. Channel strip

Sends and Returns

N/a

Panning

Centre

Fader

−3.7db

Output

Master

Plugins Expanded

9. Drum replacer

Mix	100 per cent wet
Decay	Short

Having set up the real snare channels we'll now turn our attention to the samples we will blend with the original hits. Just as with the kick drum, we are going to employ three different samples, each with its own distinct character. The first plugin on this channel is therefore a drum replacer to trigger your first sample. I like this sample to give power to the low end of the snare. Locate and load your sample of choice and set the mix to 100 per cent whilst still keeping the decay short.

Plugins Expanded

10. Channel strip

Filter	
LPF	8kHz

Equalizer			
+10db	200Hz	Bell shape	Medium Q
+9db	300Hz	Bell shape	Medium Q
+3db	4.5kHz	Bell shape	Widest Q
+10db	5kHz	Bell shape	Medium Q

Compressor	
Threshold	0
Attack	Fast
Release	Fast
Ratio	3:1
Attenuation	3db max

Now insert a channel strip plugin and dial in the setting shown previously. Again, we are rolling off the top end; then boosting big to get some weight. There is no such thing as too big of a boost in my opinion; that's the most common problem most people have when shaping sounds – under equalizing. I crank the knobs up until I like what I hear, not what I see or what I've been told. Innovation equals excellence, that's how new techniques and sounds emerge.

There is nothing special happening on the compressor, just a gentle go-to setting lowering the peaks by 3db max.

CHANNEL 8: SNARE SAMPLE B

Insert a new track/channel and name it 'Mid'.

Insert Fx

11. Drum replacer
12. Channel strip

Sends and Returns

N/a

Panning

Centre

Fader

−6.5db

Output

Master

Plugins Expanded

11. Drum replacer

Mix	100 per cent wet
Decay	Short

Insert plugin no. 11 and here sits the drum replacer once more to trigger your second snare-drum sample. You are probably one step ahead of me here from the name of the channel, but my sample of choice, you've guessed it, fills the mid-range area of the snare drum. Locate and load your sample and set the mix to 100 per cent so only the sample is heard and keep the decay short.

Plugins Expanded

12. Channel strip

Filter	
HPF	30Hz
LPF	18kHz

Equalizer			
+7.9db	178Hz	Bell shape	Medium Q
+11.4db	574Hz	Bell shape	Medium Q
+7.1db	4kHz	Bell shape	Medium Q
+8.8db	10kHz	Bell shape	Medium Q

Compressor	
Threshold	−16.9
Attack	Fast
Release	Medium
Ratio	4:1

Expander/gate	
Threshold	−48db
Range	−60db
Attack	5.0
Release	250.0
Hold	10.0
Ratio	4.0

The next plugin to insert is a channel strip – plugin no. 12. Throw it on and dial it in. There is some serious sound shaping going on here, don't fear the boost! Remember we are going to be blending this sample with another two samples as well as the original snare drum so we can have some fun here. It is very important that each sample cuts through with its own unique character so we're chopping the top and tails off with filters and pushing the EQ curve way up to give it an identity. There is compression and a gate on this one too.

CHANNEL 9: SNARE SAMPLE C

Insert a new track/channel and name it 'High'.

Insert Fx

13. Drum replacer

14. Transient designer

Sends and Returns

N/a

Panning

Centre

Fader

−3.4db

Output

Master

Plugins Expanded
13. Drum replacer

Mix	100 per cent wet
Decay	Short

Insert plugin no. 13 – the drum replacer – to trigger your third snare sample. With this one I like to accentuate the high range of the snare drum. Locate and load your high sample and set the mix to 100 per cent so only the sample is heard, and remember to keep the decay short.

Plugins Expanded
14. Transient designer

Attack	+15db
Sustain	0
Output gain	+5db

Plugin no. 14 is a transient designer. Insert one now. Any transient designer will do, although some work better than others. Try a few demos and blind test the best against the freebies. One that is

aimed at rhythmic elements would be awesome. Each transient designer will have slightly differing controls, but basically they amplify or attenuate the initial attack of a sound (the transient) and sustain may be shortened or prolonged too. As you can see, I'm bringing the initial attack of my snare hit up by 15db to add crack and snap.

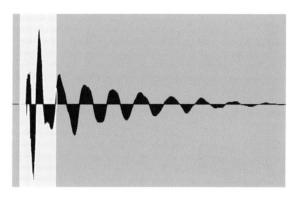

A 'transient', in musical terms, is the initial high energy peak found at the beginning of a sound.

Transients contain a great deal of useful information that can be shaped creatively using a transient designer plugin.

CHANNEL 10: SNARE REVERB SAMPLE

Insert a new stereo track/channel and name it 'VERB'.

Insert Fx

15. Drum replacer

Sends and Returns

N/a

Panning

Centre

Fader

+6.7db

Output

Master

Plugins Expanded
15. Drum replacer

Mix	100 per cent wet

The next plugin in our template is a drum replacer. This is an unusual one as it contains a snare reverb sample, rather than the sound of the drum itself. The drum replacer settings are straightforward enough; just make sure the mix dial is set to 100 per cent wet so that only the sample is heard.

The reverb sample I use comes from a sample library, but it's easy and fun to make your own; just fire a snare hit through a reverb plugin with the mix parameter set to 100 per cent and record the output.

Your sample is triggered by a feed from the original snare performance, the same performance that all the other snare samples are triggered by, so everything is always perfectly aligned.

I find this is the best way to have a controlled snare reverb hit every mix, every time. If you're making your own, then roll off the top and bottom frequencies to ensure it doesn't swamp the real snare and take some time to get it perfect. Then forget about it and stick with it forevermore. It's one less thing to think about, just blend it in with the channel fader to taste.

CHANNEL 11: HI-HAT
Insert a new track/channel and name it 'HT06'.

Insert Fx
16. Limiter/maximizer
17. Equalizer

Sends and Returns
N/a

Panning
Centre

Fader
+0.4db

Output
Master

Plugins Expanded
16. Limiter/maximizer

Threshold	–13.7db
Output ceiling	–0.5db
Attenuation	–3db max

Moving on to the hi-hat channel and plugin no. 16, I use a limiter/maximizer as the first plugin in the chain to level out the hi-hat hits. I do it this way round because I want to be able to EQ the sound after it is smoothed out, and not before. So, go ahead and insert your limiter/maximizer.

If, like me, you are using a limiter/maximizer designed with mastering in mind there will generally be a dithering stage. Dithering is the process used to reduce bit length in the most pleasing way possible. This is usually only applied during mixdown to 16 bits. However, I have to say I never mess with the dithering settings; these sound awesome as they are. I stick to the default setting (24 bits, type 1, normal), which is one less thing to think about.

Plugins Expanded
17. Equalizer

HPF	754Hz		
–6.72db	830Hz	Bell shape	Wide Q
+7.49db	9.5kHz	Bell shape	Narrow/medium Q

Plugin no. 17 is an equalizer. There is not much good going on down low with the hi-hat, so we're rolling off the low end with a high-pass filter and doubling up the attenuation with bell-shaped curve. Then it's a boost for the good stuff at 9.5kHz where the metallic air breathes.

CHANNEL 12: TOM TOM 1

Insert a new track/channel and name it 'Tom 1'.

Insert Fx

18. Drum replacer

19. Equalizer

Sends and Returns

N/a

Panning

53 per cent left

Fader

0db

Output

Master

Plugins Expanded
18. Drum replacer

Mix	Blend to taste

Yes, plugin no. 18 is the good old drum replacer once more, but before you skip on by there is a difference here. With the tom toms, as with the snare, I like to blend the samples with the original sound. Whereas we kept the snare sound separate from the samples to give us the freedom of riding up the original hits, I don't do that with the toms. I don't see that it's necessary, so the original hits and samples can be managed within the convenience of this one plugin. So, go ahead and insert your drum replacer and locate and load your samples. How much you blend the samples with the real drum is up to you. I often ride up the level of the real toms when my drum replacer is having trouble picking out a roll or maybe when I just want to confuse the listener into thinking, 'How did he do that!?'

If you are placing the samples by hand just run them alongside the real hits on separate tracks.

Plugins Expanded
19. Equalizer

+5.6db	128Hz	Bell shape	Medium Q
–5.6db	490Hz	Bell shape	Medium/narrow Q
–11.6db	802Hz	Bell shape	Medium Q
+7.2db	15kHz	Bell shape	Wide Q

Plugin no. 19 is an equalizer once more with four bands replicating a standard go-to curve for tom toms, so insert your EQ and dial them in. All we are doing is putting some weight and air behind those hits whilst taking away some of the less pleasing low mid frequencies.

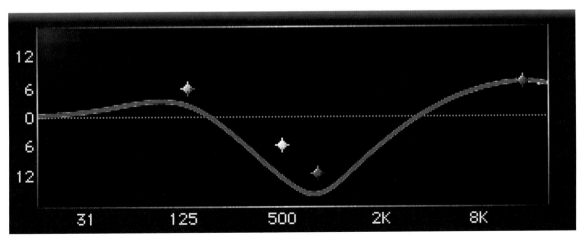

I love this classic Tom EQ curve. I use it on all three TOM channels.

CHANNEL 13: TOM TOM 2
Insert a new track/channel and name it 'Tom 2'.

Insert Fx
20. Drum replacer
21. Equalizer

Sends and Returns
N/a

Panning
Centre

Fader
0db

Output
Master

Plugins Expanded

As per Tom 1

The plugins for the second tom tom channel are identical to the first so insert your two plugins, dial in your EQ settings, locate and load your samples and you're good to go.

CHANNEL 14: TOM TOM 3
Insert a new track/channel and name it 'Tom 3'.

Insert Fx
22. Drum replacer
23. Equalizer

Sends and Returns
N/a

Panning
57 per cent right

Fader
0db

Output
Master

Plugins Expanded

As per Tom 1

Nice and easy again. The third tom tom channel is identical to the first two so again insert your two plugins, dial in your EQ settings and locate and load your samples. If you need more than three tom-tom channels simply duplicate one or more, load your new replacement samples and use the same EQ settings.

CHANNEL 15: OVERHEAD MICROPHONE LEFT
Insert a new track/channel and name it 'OH L'.

Insert Fx
24. Channel strip

Sends and Returns
N/a

Panning
100 per cent left

Fader
+7.9db

Output
Master

Plugins Expanded
24. Channel strip

Filter	
HPF	350Hz

Equalizer			
–6db	1kHz	Bell shape	Narrow/medium Q
+9db	10kHz	Shelf	

Compressor	
Threshold	+7
Attack	Fast
Release	Fast
Ratio	3:1

There is just one plugin on this channel – plugin no. 24 – a channel strip. I'm using the high-pass filter, EQ and compression stages to shape the audio. I don't care for much room sound in my overheads so I use a high-pass filter to get rid of what I call the trash. The EQ is then performing a corrective cut while adding air with a shelf starting at 10kHz. You will notice I've set the compressor to a fast attack so it will grab any cymbal crashes and level them out. I then use the make-up gain to replace the dip in volume.

CHANNEL 16: OVERHEAD MICROPHONE RIGHT
Insert a new track/channel and name it 'OH R'.

Insert Fx
25. Channel strip

Sends and Returns
N/a

Panning
100 per cent right

Fader
+7.9db

Output
Master

Plugins Expanded

As per OH L

The overhead right channel is identical to the overhead left channel in every way except for the panning, so go ahead and copy the previous channel strip.

One interesting point regarding the panning of drums (and the piano) that always gets asked is: 'Do you pan elements from the perspective of the drummer or audience?' Well, it is all personal taste, of course, but most mix engineers, myself included, seem to place the drums as they would appear to the drummer (i.e. the first tom on the left, the second in the centre and the third on the right) as if you were sat on the drummer's stool looking out at the audience. There is no right or wrong, unless you are layering samples on top of a live performance. Then it is vital to match the panning of the samples to the actual placement of drums as captured by the stereo microphones. Listen carefully and the overheads will reveal all.

CHANNEL 17: ROOM MICROPHONE
Insert a new stereo track/channel and name it 'Room'.

Insert Fx
26. Reverb

Sends and Returns
N/a

Panning
Centre

Fader
+1.4db

Output
Master

Plugins Expanded
26. Reverb

Reverb	
Room size	499m^3
Decay time	0.6 seconds
Pre-delay	39.9ms

EQ		
–3db	1.6kHz	Shelf

Plugin no. 26 is a plugin of the reverberation type. I've included the settings common to all reverbs here; look in the back at Appendix B should you wish to know which brand I favour. This is a drum room preset. I love presets. What's not to love? They save hours of initial tweaking and I leave them set the same every time. Set, leave, quick mix and get on with living! Be careful when entering the room size as the size I have included is in cubic metres. If your reverb only allows metres you will have to do a bit of head-

scratching and calculator tapping or you'll have one very big room.

You may wonder why I'm putting a reverb plugin that emulates the sound of a room on a channel that contains a room sound! For me this is a way of adding more depth to a mix, by making the room bigger and having control over its size and response. You can use this on the overheads too to make them larger than life. Just be careful of the decay time. I set mine to 0.8 seconds maximum; any longer and the reverb starts to get 'spitty' on the cymbals and the hi-hats.

Careful selection of the right preset can take a dry and lifeless space and transform it into a quality, realistic fake environment that can fool listening ears.

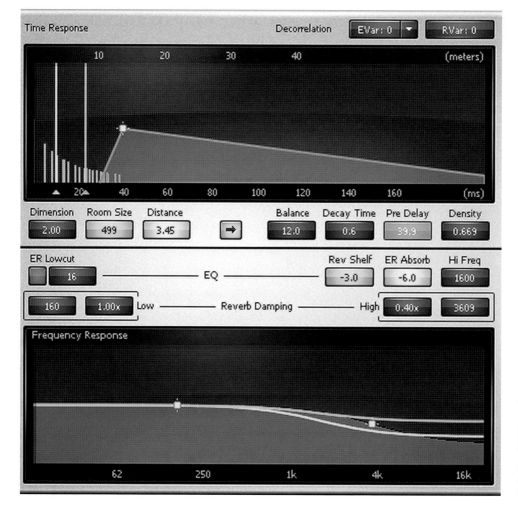

A reverberation plugin is the perfect tool to add an additional room ambience.

CHANNEL 18: TAMBOURINE
Insert a new track/channel and name it 'Tamb'.

Insert Fx
27. Limiter/maximizer

Sends and Returns
N/a

Panning
Centre

Fader
–5db

Output
Master

Plugins Expanded
27. Limiter/maximizer

Threshold	–10db
Out ceiling	0db
Release	1.0

Insert a limiter/maximizer to smooth out the tambourine and make it louder. I use this for all the percussion elements, just to smooth them out and big them up.

THE DRUM SECTION BUSSES

Channel 19 – the drum submix buss dry channel – marks the end of the individual drums and represents our first steps into stereo busses. We're on the road that will lead us to that professional drum sound, taking in parallel compression along the way. If you're not familiar with the terms 'submix', 'buss' or 'parallel compression', now is the time to dig deep into your DAW manual. These busses will all receive our live drums and samples as we unify them and shape them into one cohesive sound.

For the present moment though let's concentrate on finishing setting the remaining channels of the drum section. We will then turn our attention to

the routing, including the specifics of our parallel compression layout.

CHANNEL 19: DRUM BUSS DRY
Insert a new stereo track/channel/buss and name it 'DS Dry'.

Insert Fx
N/a

Sends and Returns
N/a

Panning
Centre

Fader
+2.5db

Output
Master

As the title of the channel suggests this is a mix buss that will receive the drums sent to it and pass them on to their destination without any processing whatsoever, so no plugins here.

CHANNEL 20: DRUM BUSS PARALLEL COMPRESSION
Insert a new stereo track/channel/buss and name it 'DS PC'.

Insert Fx
28. Compressor

Sends and Returns
N/a

Panning
Centre

Fader
–3.7db

Output
Master

Plugins Expanded
28. Compressor

Threshold	–28db
Ratio	10:1
Attack	Fast
Release	Fast
Make-up	0

To achieve parallel compression, a wet compressed signal must be added to the dry unaffected signal. This can be handled totally within a plugin by using the incorporated mix dial to vary the amount of compression applied, or by creating a second channel to form the wet compressed signal as we are doing here. Either way, it is the amount of compressed signal that you add back into the original signal that counts. Experiment with varying degrees of blend. One point to note though – it is important to keep the two signals in sample-accurate synchronicity. If either one becomes misaligned, phase cancellation will occur and weaken the effect.

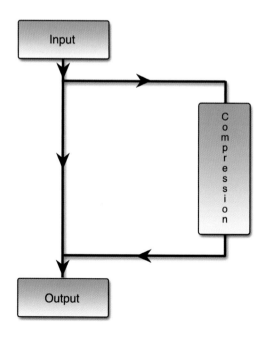

Parallel compression involves blending a dry, 'clean' signal with a wet 'compressed' signal.

Channel 20, therefore, gives us our parallel compression. It blends with the previous dry channel to create an effect that brings punch to the kick and snare drums. I am using one compressor here so insert a compressor too and dial in the settings. You can see from the low threshold, high ratio and fast reaction times that this is designed to add a 'slammed' sound. It's jumping on anything that passes through it and hammering the unsuspecting audio down deep and fast.

Lately I have been setting this channel higher than I have previously as I'm shooting for a more compressed, snappy, aggressive sound.

Regarding the fader levels, it's really important to view the fader settings of my template as starting positions. The ratio of compressed to dry signal will vary greatly and depend on the type of processor you are using and how much compression is taking place. Always go with your instincts and set everything to your own personal taste.

CHANNEL 21: DRUM SUBMIX
Insert a new stereo track/channel/buss and name it 'DS11'.

Insert Fx
29. Compressor
30. Analogue channel emulation
31. Limiter
32. Clipper
33. Equalizer

Sends and Returns
N/a

Panning
Centre

Fader
+8db

Output
Master

Plugins Expanded
29. Compressor

Threshold	−5.4db
Ratio	2:1
Attack	0.27ms
Release	66.6ms

This is a significant channel. It's the main destination for every drum sound and submix channel that doesn't go direct to the master channel.
Everything else comes through here. We've got
five plugins to work through, the first being a
compressor, so grab your favourite tool and throw
it on.

I like to keep the compression ratio to 2:1 in
order to keep as much of the dynamics as possible, while still smoothing it out and giving 'that
sound' that drums sound like on records. I use
a lot of compressors, but use just a little bit from
each one and I never hit any one of them too hard
but rather let a bunch of little compressions sum
up to one big sound. That's how mixes can sound
loud and dynamic at the same time.

Plugins Expanded
30. Analogue channel emulation

Drive	0
Compression	5.8
Attack	0.18
Release	241
Output	−5.5

The second plugin is an analogue amplifier emulation that works by smoothing out transients in true
analogue fashion. I've included the settings from
my template just in case you own the same plugin
as me (see Appendix B). Any tape saturation
or analogue amplifier/channel emulation plugin
should do fine. Push it just enough to compress
the transients a little.

Plugins Expanded
31. Limiter

Output ceiling	−4db
Gain	+12db

Plugin no. 31 is a limiter. My limiter has just two
dials on it – an output ceiling and gain control.
Yours may also have two as there is not much else
a limiter can do. Just increase the gain to push
the signal into the threshold (the output ceiling) to
limit the output. I see this as a light limiter – there's
nothing too heavy-handed here. The output has
been reduced to correctly gain stage the chain
and not distort the next plugin.

Plugins Expanded
32. Clipper

25 per cent (3 lights)

Plugin no. 32 is a clipper type. This adds presence, making the drums seem louder without
changing their sound. A good peak clipper will
preserve the transients and add to the boldness of
the source. The benefit of a peak clipper over limiting or compressing and turning up the output is
cleaner sound with fewer side effects. Whichever
clipper you choose, look to increase the power
of the source by around 25 per cent (that's three
lights on my choice of plugin) without increasing
the actual gain.

Plugins Expanded
33. Equalizer

HPF	50Hz

Plugin no. 33 is an equalizer and although I'm
documenting this one it is fair to say that I rarely
use it. Most of the time it sits disabled in the chain
watching the beats fly by. The only time I will
switch it on is if the song I'm mixing has some
deep bass synth sounds or similar going on. Only

then will I pull in the high-pass filter and take away some of the really low frequencies that only cause problems.

CHANNEL 22: SNARE DRUM PARALLEL COMPRESSION

Insert a new track/channel/buss and name it 'SNR Par'.

Insert Fx

34. Clipper
35. Compressor
36. Equalizer

Sends and Returns

N/a

Panning

Centre

Fader

+4.8

Output

Master

Plugins Expanded
34. Clipper

45 per cent (5 lights)

Channel no. 22 is a parallel compression buss solely for the snare-drum samples – nothing else. I don't know how you'd get that snare sound without parallel compression. When I take it off it sounds to me like someone's thrown a wet towel over the drum. My first plugin for this channel is a clipper, just to make it loud. I'm hitting it pretty hard – you want some serious power added here.

Plugins Expanded
35. Compressor

Input	0db
Threshold	–42db
Ratio	3.5:1
Attack	35ms
Release	100ms
Make-up gain	5.2db

Plugin no. 35 is a compressor – insert one now. This just locks in the 'crack' for me. Look for yours to do the same. Focus on getting the same 'crack' that cuts through when blended back in with the other snares.

Plugins Expanded
36. Equalizer

+8db	250Hz	Narrow/medium Q
+3db	550Hz	Medium Q
+15db	9.13kHz	Wide/medium Q

Our final plugin on this channel – and the last plugin within the drum section – is an equalizer. This just adds a little extra EQ to get us where we need to be on the parallel compression for the samples. Don't be afraid to keep equalizing until you get where you want to be sound-wise.

Now we have set up the drums section, all we need to do is route the channels to their final destinations.

THE DRUM SECTION: ROUTING AND GROUPING

Until now we have ignored each channel's auxiliary sends and returns and output destinations and left them in their default state. But having set up the individual channels and busses and familiarized ourselves with them, we can now complete the final routing by referencing the following grid.

Within a DAW almost any output can be sent to

any input. The output of each channel is listed vertically on the left; the inputs run horizontally across the top.

Note that only eight channels will remain routed to the master out – all other channels must be deactivated from the master channel.

So, to take the first J-KIK channel as an example: if you were to take a ruler and follow a line from the J-KIK output on the left all the way across the inputs to the far right, you will see that the only destinations for the J-KIK outputs are the inputs of DS Dry and DS PC (don't forget to disconnect it from the master buss).

Follow this process, one by one, to route all the outputs to the inputs denoted by each X.

If a routing grid is new to you, it is as simple as working through the channels listed down the left-hand column and looking for the X that links the output of a specific channel to the input of another.

	Master In	J-KIK	D-KIK	H-KIK	Cym Rev	SNR Top	SNR Bot	Fatty	Mid	High	Verb	HT06	Tom 1	Tom 2	Tom 3	OH L	OH R	Room	Tamb	DS Dry	DS PC	DS11	SNR Par
Master Out																							
J-KIK																				X	X		
D-KIK																				X	X		
H-KIK																				X	X		
Cym Rev	X																						
SNR Top																				X	X		
SNR Bot																				X	X		
Fatty											X									X	X		X
Mid																				X	X		X
High																				X	X		X
Verb	X																						
HT06	X																						
Tom 1																				X	X		
Tom 2																				X	X		
Tom 3																				X	X		
OH L	X																						
OH R	X																						
Room	X																						
Tamb	X																						
DS Dry																						X	
DS PC																						X	
DS11	X																						
SNR Par																						X	

	Master In	J-KIK	D-KIK	H-KIK	Cym Rev	SNR Top	SNR Bot	Fatty	Mid	High	Verb	HT06	Tom 1	Tom 2	Tom 3	OH L	OH R	Room	Tamb	DS Dry	DS PC	DS11	SNR Par
Master Out																							
J-KIK																				X	X		
D-KIK																				X	X		
H-KIK																				X	X		
Cym Rev	X																						
SNR Top																				X	X		
SNR Bot																				X	X		
Fatty											X									X	X		X
Mid																				X	X		X
High																				X	X		X
Verb	X																						
HT06	X																						
Tom 1																				X	X		
Tom 2																				X	X		
Tom 3																				X	X		
OH L	X																						
OH R	X																						
Room	X																						
Tamb	X																						
DS Dry																						X	
DS PC																						X	
DS11	X																						
SNR Par																						X	

TOP: An overview of all connections can be represented in a routing grid with the outputs on the left and the inputs across the top.

BOTTOM: This example shows the routing for the J-KIK channel in which the output is routed to the input of the channels DS Dry and DS PC.

3

INSTRUMENTS

THE INSTRUMENTS SECTION

With the drums complete, we can now turn our attention to the instruments. Within my template I have created channels for all the instruments that I may mix, the idea being that it is a lot easier to delete channels than spend time trying to create them from scratch at a later date. Therefore, I recommend you set up the complete ensemble within your default template and simply discard the channels you do not use on a song by song basis.

CHANNEL 23: BASS GUITAR
Insert a new track/channel and name it 'Bass'.

Insert Fx
37. Equalizer
38. Bass enhancer

Sends and Returns
N/a

Panning
Centre

Fader
+12db

Output
Master

Plugins Expanded
37. Equalizer

HPF	80Hz		
+2db	100Hz	Bell shape	Medium Q
–20db	2kHz	Bell shape	Medium Q

Much of the music I mix is country music, and with country music I like to cut the 2kHz region because all I want the bass guitar to do is hold down the low end. Listeners of a country song like a dull bass and it is very important that every mix is true to the traditions of each individual style of music. Every listener will be conditioned to hear the specific sounds that define the genre in question, whether they are aware of it or not. It is those sounds that you've got to find and deliver to appear consistent and valid. For instance, if I want the bass guitar to stand out in a rock song then I'll boost 2kHz instead. In fact, the 2kHz frequency allows for a lot of versatility in many different genres. Another good example is this: if mixing a metal song I would boost 2kHz and then add a guitar amp simulator to make it really growl. But whatever genre I'm mixing I always keep all the other settings the same, i.e. I'll always set the high-pass filter at around 80Hz and add a bump of 100Hz; I just treat 2kHz differently.

Plugins Expanded
38. Bass Enhancer

Input	0db
Original bass	–10.4db
Enhanced bass	0.9db
Crossover frequency	80Hz

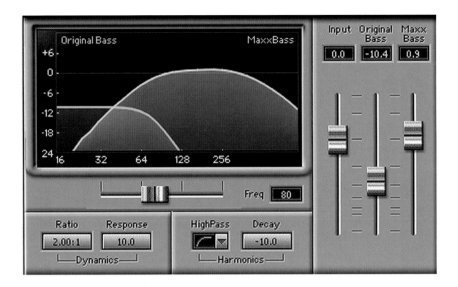

A bass enhancer is a useful tool for increasing perceived bass response, especially when audio is played via small speakers.

If you have access to a bass enhancement plugin then I've included the most relevant settings here. Each brand of plugin will vary but basically they all work by exploiting the laws of psycho-acoustics and will enhance the bass frequencies by both reinforcing existing frequencies and creating additional desirable ones.

You will have seen from my EQ settings that I always set a high-pass filter to around 80Hz or so. The purpose of the bass enhancer is to fill up the space we created with our EQ filter using the synthesized frequencies it produces.

For me, it just feels better this way. I always like to sit my bass guitar above my kick drum, without exception. Using this method, the bass and kick always sit right; by cutting off the real bass guitar at 80Hz space is created for the bass drum, which generally gets a boost around 60Hz. Then, filling in the sub 60Hz with controlled, synthesized bass guitar enhancement is perfect.

You will note that the crossover frequency of the bass enhancer is set to the same 80Hz as our high-pass filter to further define the point that real frequencies end and new, enhanced frequencies are added. However, this is a simplified statement (as bass enhancers will double up existing frequencies and the shape of crossover and filter slopes all have a bearing on exactly which frequencies are being manipulated) so always

trust your ears. The goal is to create a smooth, warm, balanced bass response, not more bass than is appropriate.

Low-frequency content that would normally be lost on small speakers is particularly well suited to being synthetically reproduced, giving the listener the impression that they are still present.

CHANNEL 24: ACOUSTIC GUITAR LEFT
Insert a new track/channel and name it 'AG L'.

Insert Fx

39. Equalizer

40. Compressor

41. Limiter/maximizer

Sends and Returns

N/a

Panning

100 per cent left

Fader

–3.2db

Output

Master

Plugins Expanded
39. Equalizer

HPF	125Hz		
−6.14db	234.24Hz	Bell shape	Narrow Q
LPF	12.36kHz		

This EQ setting is awesome for a clear and transparent acoustic guitar that cuts through a full mix. It sits well with electric guitars and a full band arrangement. We are taking out the unwanted low-end rumble with an HPF, cutting the muddy trash and trimming the top end down.

Alternatively, if I have space in the mix and a great acoustic guitar sound off tape, I'll simply add 6db at 100Hz and 5kHz (peaking EQ – med Q) to boost the low and add some presence. I'll then insert a clipper or a limiter/maximizer plugin to make it loud.

Plugins Expanded
40. Compressor

Input	−28db
Output	−18db
Attack	Medium – slow
Release	Fastest
Ratio	4:1

The compressor I use for this channel is modelled on the original 'Black Face' 1176 peak limiter. See Appendix B for my particular brand, but any compressor/limiter with 1176 or 76 in the description will be good, or you can choose any that suits your taste. Although the original 1176 was marketed as a limiting amplifier, when used at a ratio of 4:1 it acts as a compressor. This particular compressor adds darkness and softens the acoustic guitar; look for yours to do the same. The 1176 is a levelling compressor so you can hit these pretty hard.

Plugins Expanded
41. Limiter/maximizer

Threshold	−4db
Output ceiling	0db
Release	Auto release
Attenuation	No more than −3db max

All we are doing here is controlling the peaks of the track with a brick-wall limiter and maximizing the loudness. Many brick-wall limiters are classed as mastering limiters but we can use one here. I love what this does to the acoustic guitar, just makes it nice and fat. So look to add a brick-wall limiter to add some warmth and thicken the source, whilst limiting those troublesome peaks.

CHANNEL 25: ACOUSTIC GUITAR RIGHT
Insert a new track/channel and name it 'AG R'.

Insert Fx
42. Equalizer
43. Compressor
44. Limiter/maximizer

Sends and Returns
N/a

Panning
100 per cent right

Fader
−3.2db

Output
Master

Plugins Expanded

As per AG L

All the plugins on the right acoustic guitar channel are identical to those on the previous left channel; just copy them across and move the pan control all the way to the right.

CHANNEL 26: ELECTRIC GUITAR 1 LEFT
Insert a new track/channel and name it 'EG 1 L'.

Insert Fx
45. Equalizer
46. Clipper
47. Limiter/maximizer

Sends and Returns
N/a

Panning
100 per cent left

Fader
+0.7db

Output
Master

Plugins Expanded
45. Equalizer

+2.1db	100Hz	Shelf	
+1.8db	240Hz	Bell shape	Medium Q
+4.5db	7kHz	Shelf	

This is just a cool EQ curve that sounds great on electric guitars. My EQ of choice is an old-style, easy-to-use EQ with overlapping bands for sweetening; the sort of EQ that wouldn't look out of place on a guitar amp. Choose your unit and dial it in. I use this on all the electric guitar channels; they all share the same make-up so why not?

Plugins Expanded
46. Clipper

25 per cent (3 lights)

I love to insert a transparent peak clipper between the EQ and the main brick-wall peak limiter/maximizer. For me this just gives a touch more presence, making the track louder without changing the sound. A good peak clipper will preserve the transients and add to the boldness of the source. The benefit of a peak clipper over limiting or compressing and turning up the output is cleaner sound with fewer side effects. Whichever clipper you choose, look to increase the power of the source by around 25 per cent – on my choice of plugin that's three lights.

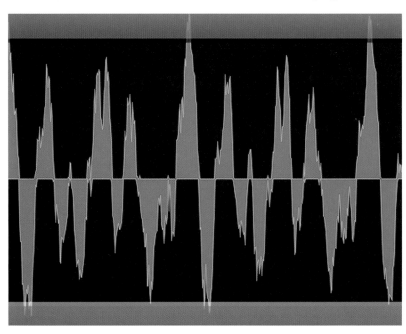

The shaded area of this waveform is clipped.

When an audio waveform is said to be 'clipped', the top arc of the waveform is not accurately reproduced, but instead represented by a straight horizontal line of samples. This happens when an audio signal is pushed beyond the maximum capability of its carrier. The clipping of audio is generally to be avoided, but when handled correctly by a plugin designed specifically for the task, clipping can add extra loudness and presence to a sound source with fewer side effects than more traditional methods.

Plugins Expanded
47. Limiter/maximizer

Threshold	−4db
Output ceiling	−0.4db
Release	Auto release
Attenuation	No more than −3db max

All we are doing is controlling the peaks of the track to maximize the loudness.

CHANNEL 27: ELECTRIC GUITAR 1 RIGHT
Insert a new track/channel and name it 'EG 1 R'.

Insert Fx
48. Equalizer
49. Clipper
50. Limiter/maximizer

Sends and Returns
N/a

Panning
100 per cent right

Fader
+0.7db

Output
Master

Plugins Expanded

As per EG 1 L

The plugins on the first right electric guitar channel are identical to those on the first left channel, with the panning set to 100 per cent right.

CHANNEL 28: ELECTRIC GUITAR 2 LEFT
Insert a new track/channel and name it 'EG 2 L'.

Insert Fx
51. Equalizer
52. Limiter/maximizer

Sends and Returns
N/a

Panning
100 per cent left

Fader
0db

Output
Master

Plugins Expanded

As per EG 1 L, but with the clipper removed

These plugins are identical to the previous electric guitar channels with one exception: I've removed the clipper. The EQ and limiter remain the same.

CHANNEL 29: ELECTRIC GUITAR 2 RIGHT

Insert a new track/channel and name it 'EG 2 R'.

Insert Fx

53. Equalizer

54. Limiter/maximizer

Sends and Returns

N/a

Panning

100 per cent right

Fader

0db

Output

Master

Plugins Expanded

As per EG 1 L, but with the clipper removed

Again, the channel follows the same pattern as the second left electric guitar channel, i.e. two plugins remain the same as the first electric guitar channel, but the clipper has been removed and panning is to the right. So, copy the previous plugins and switch the pan.

CHANNEL 30: STEEL GUITAR

Insert a new track/channel and name it 'Steel'.

Insert Fx

55. Equalizer

56. Limiter/maximizer

Sends and Returns

N/a

Panning

47 per cent left

Fader

−2.8db

Output

Master

Plugins Expanded
55. Equalizer

+3.26db	125Hz	Bell shape	Narrow – medium Q
−2.88db	224Hz	Bell shape	Narrow – medium Q
+8.45db	11.38kHz	Bell shape	Narrow – medium Q

Three bands of peaking EQ are used to boost the bass, take away some mud and add air. Find the most transparent EQ you can as you don't want to colour the sound at all when equalizing steel guitars or, in fact, any sound that is always represented in a very natural way.

The term 'transparent' can be used to describe any audio process path or circuit that leaves the original sound as intact as possible. Ultimate transparency can be thought of as a sound passing through a circuit without there being any noticeable difference at the output stage. If a difference is perceived and the original sound is changed in some way, the changes are called colour. Varying degrees of colour are added throughout the recording, mixing and mastering process. Train your ears to become sensitive to colour as it can be a powerful tool when used carefully. As a matter that is subjective to the individual listener, it can be thought of as good or bad, intentional or unintentional or, more often than not, not thought of at all!

Plugins Expanded
56. Limiter/maximizer

Threshold	−5db
Output ceiling	0db
Release	Auto release
Attenuation	No more than −3db max

Insert your limiter/maximizer for extra fullness and loudness.

CHANNEL 31: B3 ORGAN
Insert a new stereo track/channel and name it 'B3'.

Insert Fx
57. Equalizer
58. Limiter/maximizer

Sends and Returns
N/a

Panning
Centre

Fader
−2.8db

Output
Master

Plugins Expanded
57. Equalizer

+2.30db	125Hz	Bell shape	Narrow – medium Q
−4.61db	218Hz	Bell shape	Narrow – medium Q
+4.22db	5.17kHz	Bell shape	Narrow – medium Q
+7.68db	12.02kHz	Bell shape	Narrow – medium Q

I like to use this one EQ curve for all the pianos, organs and real keyboard sounds; they all live in the same frequency range so why not?

Plugins Expanded
58. Limiter/maximizer

Threshold	−4db
Output ceiling	0db
Release	Auto release
Attenuation	No more than −3db max

Then add the limiter/maximizer to big up the sound.

CHANNEL 32: PIANO
Insert a new stereo track/channel and name it 'Piano'.

Insert Fx
59. Equalizer
60. Limiter/maximizer

Sends and Returns
N/a

Panning
Centre

Fader
+3.7db

Output
Master

Plugins Expanded

As per B3 ORGAN

Both these plugins are the same for the piano as they were for the B3. You can use this channel set-up for any of your keyboard sounds.

CHANNEL 33: SYNTHESIZER 1
Insert a new stereo track/channel and name it 'Synth 1'.

Insert Fx
61. Equalizer
62. Limiter/maximizer

Sends and Returns
N/a

Panning
Centre

Fader
−7.5db

Output
Master

Plugins Expanded

As per B3 ORGAN

This is the same equalizer curve and loudness maximizer as for the organ and piano channels. It works for me and my music. Don't be afraid to change the EQ to suit your own style though – never give up until you find the right sound.

CHANNEL 34: SYNTHESIZER 2

Insert a new stereo track/channel and name it 'Synth 2'.

Insert Fx
63. Equalizer
64. Limiter/maximizer

Sends and Returns
N/a

Panning
Centre

Fader
–12.8db

Output
Master

Plugins Expanded

As per B3 ORGAN

Once more, as per the previous three channels, all these settings are good for your keyboard sounds so just copy them across.

THE INSTRUMENT SECTION BUSSES

CHANNEL 35: INSTRUMENT DELAY BUSS

Insert a new stereo track/channel/buss and name it 'I Delay'.

Insert Fx
65. Delay

Sends and Returns
N/a

Panning
Centre

Fader
0db

Output
Master

Plugins Expanded
65. Delay

Decay time	*233 milliseconds (ms)
Tempo	Set to tempo of track
Delay	Eighth notes
Feedback	25 per cent
Mix	100 per cent

* I've included the decay time from my template but set this to represent an eighth note delay in milliseconds in relation to the tempo of your track.

This is the first appearance of our time-based delay plugin. It is placed on its own buss, which means we can route anything we like to it. The mix dial is set to 100 per cent so that only the affected sound is replayed. It's awesome for guitars and in fact is identical to the delay we will place in the vocal section later. I separate them out so I have control over them individually, but the settings are the same. Set the delay time to corre-

There are a multitude of choices when it comes to time-based effects.

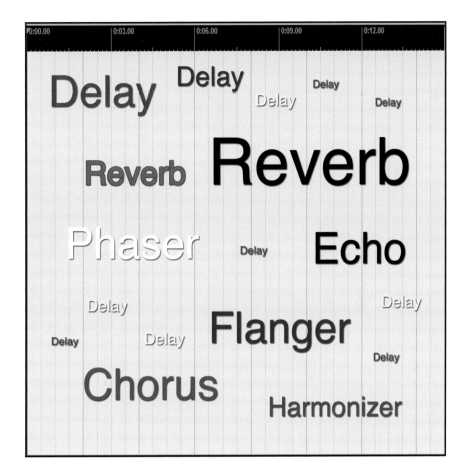

spond to your project tempo and you're good to go. This is actually a preset called 'memory man'; you may well have the same preset as it shows up on many delay units. Don't fear the preset. I love using presets and will always go to a preset rather than spend precious mixing time tweaking settings.

It is important to know how the effect you are working on sounds; only then can you judge how it will blend with your complete song. Listen to the effect in isolation and then use it sparingly as too much can drown a mix. Regarding time-based effects (reverbs, delays, flangers, phasers, doublers, etc.), I don't use that many. I like to keep the mix clean. Throughout our template you will notice we are only using one reverb snare sample, one delay (duplicated for instruments and vocals), one doubler and two reverbs – that's it!

CHANNEL 36: INSTRUMENT REVERB BUSS
Insert a new stereo track/channel/buss and name it 'I Verb'.

Insert Fx
66. Reverb

Sends and Returns
N/a

Panning
Centre

Fader
+5.9db

Output
Master

Plugins Expanded
66. Reverb

Reverb type	Room
Pre-delay	0
Time	1.05 seconds
Size	76
Early reflections	Off
Mix	100 per cent wet

Reverb EQ

Frequency	100Hz
Gain	−5.0
Frequency	3kHz
Gain	+3.0

I use this reverb for all my instruments. It sounds good to me. I only use in-the-box reverbs, no outboard gear anywhere; this way I can recall 100 per cent of the mix and all the settings all of the time, every time. I've included here all the common settings that you'll find on almost any reverb, so go and find your favourite and dial them in.

Any room reverb will do, just set the time and the size with no pre-delay or early reflections, then roll off the low end (reverb's low end is a killer and will swamp your mix) and brighten the top. Make sure you are setting the mix to 100 per cent. All we want is the sound of the reverb and none of the unprocessed signal; we can use the channel fader to control the level of the reverb within the mix.

CHANNEL 37: DOUBLE TRACK
Insert a new stereo track/channel/buss and name it 'Phas'.

Insert Fx
67. Doubler

Sends and Returns
N/a

Panning
Centre

Fader
0db

Output
Master

Plugins Expanded
67. Doubler

Voice 1	
Gain	0db
Pan	−45.0
Delay	7.3ms
Feedback	0
Detune	6 cents

Voice 2	
Gain	0db
Pan	+45.0
Delay	10ms
Feedback	0
Detune	−6 cents

Mix	100 per cent wet (no original signal)

I refer to this as the 'double track' channel as I use a doubler plugin to primarily widen vocals and acoustic guitars. It's kind of like the Eventide H3000 series hardware. If you analyze the settings I'm using (which are preset of course) then you'll see that the plugin is taking two copies of the original signal, panning one left and one right, adding two different short delays and tuning voice one up and voice two down, both by 6 cents (100 cents = 1 semitone).

If you don't have a doubler plugin, don't worry. It's so easy to recreate by making two duplicate copies of your source track, panning one left and one right and adding the delays and pitch shifting as previously. You can also take this to another level by duplicating the source track four or even six times and pitching each subsequent copy up and down by 6, 12 and 18 cents respectively. I don't use it personally, but it can be a great way to thicken a lead vocal.

THE INSTRUMENT SECTION: ROUTING AND GROUPING

Awesome! Now you have set up and familiarized yourself with each channel and buss of the instrument section, you can complete the final routing as per the following grid.

Just to refresh your memory, the output of each channel is listed vertically on the left and the inputs appear horizontally across the top.

So, to take the Bass and AG L channels as examples: for the Bass, the only connection is to the master channel whilst for the AG L channel the destinations are the master, I Verb and Phas.

Follow this process to route all the outputs one by one to the inputs denoted by each X.

You will note that all the instruments stay firmly routed to the master buss, but additional routing is completed by sending a signal feed to the effects channels.

Follow the routing grid for the instrument section to connect all the relevant outputs to inputs.

	Master In	Bass	AG L	AG R	EG 1L	EG 1R	EG 2L	EG 2R	Steel	B3	Piano	Synth 1	Synth 2	I Delay	I Verb	Phas
Master Out																
Bass	X															
AG L	X														X	X
AG R	X														X	X
EG 1L	X														X	
EG 1R	X														X	
EG 2L	X													X		
EG 2R	X													X		
Steel	X													X		
B3	X														X	
Piano	X													X	X	
Synth 1	X															
Synth 2	X															
I Delay	X															
I Verb	X															
Phas	X															

4

VOCALS

THE VOCAL SECTION

Moving on to the all-important vocal section, the lead-vocal track is *the* most important aspect of any mix. It is the emotion, the melody and the song's defining voice. The vocal section itself consists of lead vocal, a cloned lead vocal and any backing vocals. Treat sampled phrases, chants and words as backing vocals and place them within this section. Even if you are currently only mixing instrumental music, I recommend you set up the vocal-section channels as you never know when they may be required.

CHANNEL 38: LEAD VOCAL 1
Insert a new track/channel and name it 'Vox 1'.

Insert Fx
68. Compressor
69. Channel strip
70. Vocal multi-effects
71. De-esser 1
72. De-esser 2

Sends and Returns
N/a

Panning
Centre

Fader
+2.5db

Output
Master

Plugins Expanded
68. Compressor

Input	−27
Output	−18
Attack	Slow
Release	Fast
Ratio	4:1
Analogue noise	Off

We start our vocal chain with a levelling compressor. The levelling compressor I use is modelled on the original 'Blue Face' 1176 peak limiter. It's important to find a levelling compressor. Any compressor/limiter with 1176 or 76 in the description will be perfect, but any leveller will suffice. You can hit these types of compressor pretty hard. They like to be compressing all the time, gently massaging the overall level to a more controlled output. Gain-reduction levels of 10–20db are not uncommon.

We are going to be adding a few stages of compression to the lead vocal but every stage brings something different to the party. Adding these multiple layers of dynamic control means the vocal sits perfectly within the mix in a way that negates any need for further fader riding or gain-stage editing. This is a major factor in a quick professional mix where many precious hours are saved.

Through compression, the loudest parts of an audio signal are reduced, bringing them closer to the quietest levels. The compressor can then boost the overall level of the signal to give a more control-

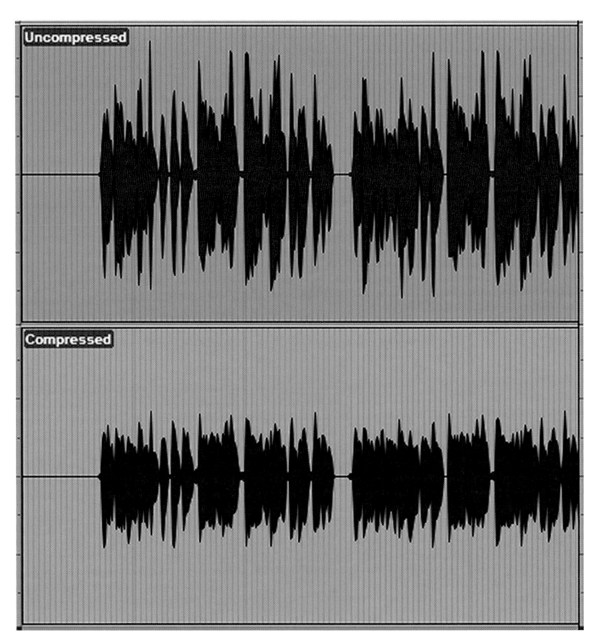

Compression works by decreasing dynamic range.

led, fuller sound. The above diagram demonstrates a lead vocal being compressed by a 1176-type levelling compressor. You can see from only this one layer of compression how much more controlled the waveform is. Think of compression as an imaginary magic finger moving the channel fader up and down. When the sound source gets too loud, the magic finger turns it down. When it gets too quiet the magic happens again and the sound source increases.

Plugins Expanded
69. Channel strip

Compressor	
Threshold	−12.48db
Ratio	2.4:1
Attack	82ms
Release	1
Gain reduction	3db max

Filter	
HPF	164Hz

EQ			
−1.73db	189Hz	Bell shape	Narrow – medium Q
−1.54db	245Hz	Bell shape	Narrow – medium Q
−0.96db	305Hz	Bell shape	Narrow – medium Q
+2.30db	15kHz	Bell shape	Medium Q

Now insert your channel strip plugin. We want to use the compression, filter and EQ sections. Four bands of EQ and a high-pass filter are recommended. If your channel strip only has three bands, which is pretty standard, just add an additional EQ.

Looking a little deeper into the settings: whereas the previous levelling compressor worked on the whole of the signal by riding the level up and down to stabilize the perceived image, this compressor works on the peaks only, reducing them by up to 3db max. The EQ is rolling off unwanted low-end rumble and surgically cutting small dips out of the muddy problem area before adding some air. I don't care who the singer is or how they've been tracked, they're always going to get some more air! These settings will need tweaking depending on your vocal talent but this will get you in the ballpark.

Regarding the Q value (the width of frequency bands affected), it is general practice to use a narrow Q when cutting and a wider, broader Q when boosting.

Plugins Expanded
70. Vocal multi-effects

Compression threshold	−18db

After levelling the waveform, clipping 3db off the loudest clips, some surgical EQ and adding a touch of air, the next processor is harder to describe. It's one of the few plugins that I can't live without. There are probably only a couple of plugins that I'd label as irreplaceable and this is one. Take a peek in Appendix B at the back of this book if you want to know which brand I use and, should you already own it, you'll know there is just one slider, which for me is always set to the magic number -18db.

Looking inside the manual of said processor, it is clear that clever use of compression, gating, limiting and level maximization is going on within this one easy-to-use unit. To recommend setting up a chain of effects to emulate this would be problematic as I couldn't be sure of the results. This wouldn't be in your best interest and wouldn't be in keeping with the ethos of this book. Therefore, my advice to you is this: gather all the vocal multi-effects processor plugins you can find and try them one by one. Test them all and ask yourself this one question: 'Does it make the track better or worse?' – it is as simple as that. Look for the one that in your opinion is better than all the others and stick with it forevermore – job done. Don't discount the freebies; there are plenty of free plugins to try as well as the usual suspects.

Plugins Expanded
71. De-esser 1

Frequency	8328Hz
Threshold	−23.8db
Attenuation	3db max

All that compression is great for controlling the dynamic of our vocal track, but compression works by turning down the loudest peaks so that the overall level of a track can be turned up; therefore, it's inevitable that certain displeasing attributes get boosted too – namely noise, breathing, clicks, pops and sibilance ('sss' or 'shh' sounds). With the first of our two de-esser plugins we are controlling the sibilance (the other attributes can be manually edited out if troublesome). So insert a de-esser and it will do exactly that, it'll grab the 'esses' and turn them down. Some work better than others, so try a few and find your favourite. You'll have to adjust the frequency dial from time to time depending on whether you're working with a male or female voice. Stay within the 8–10kHz range and you'll be fine. You only want to bang this down by a maximum of about 3db, any more and you will give the singer a lisp!

If you are not sure at what frequency the essing is happening just throw on a temporary peaking EQ with a narrow Q and boost it by 10db. Then slowly move the band up and down within the 8–10kHz range until you hit the pain! Find the pain and reduce the gain!

Plugins Expanded
72. De-esser 2

Frequency	2kHz
Threshold	−21.8db
Attenuation	3db max

Now add a second de-esser. This one acts like a de-honker to take out the nasal quality of the sound. Again, only bang it down by a maximum of about 3db. The frequency is always set at 2kHz.

Whatever style of vocal I mix, be it pop, rock, country or anything else, this chain of processors remains the same and has done for the last ten years or more.

Channel 39: Lead Vocal 2
Insert a new track/channel and name it 'Vox 2'.

Insert Fx
73. Compressor
74. Channel strip
75. Multi-effects
76. De-esser 1
77. De-esser 2

Sends and Returns
N/a

Panning
Centre

Fader
+2.5db

Output
Master

Plugins Expanded

As per Lead Vocal 1

The second lead vocal channel is a clone of the first. This is an exact copy in every way and should always remain so. If you change anything on one channel it is vital that you change it on the second cloned channel. Both channels should reinforce each other, boosting their combined energy levels. Any differences between the two will cause frequency cancellation and weaken the signal.

Any slight variation in timing between two signals will result in phase cancellation, giving a lesser sound. Two identical sounds summed together will double the combined sound energy, but flip the polarity of one channel and the two channels will cancel each other out, returning a deafening silence as the sound disappears altogether!

We can use this magic trick (often referred to as a Null Test) to check all is good; invert the polarity of one channel only using the polarity switch and

It is vital when duplicating sounds that any cloned copies be kept in sample accurate unison.

the vocal should disappear totally. If any 'phasey' remainders of the vocal exist, then there are differences between the two channels. Find the offending plugin and set them straight. You'll want to deactivate the buss effect sends momentarily while you run this test as a distant effect could be misconstrued as a problem when there isn't one. Just remember to switch them straight back on again.

I spent years trying to get my vocal to sit right before settling on this cloning method. By using it I can get the vocal right on top of the track every time. I've used this for at least the last fifteen years; every mix during that time has had a cloned lead-vocal channel.

send all our backing vocals to one submix channel where they can all be treated together as one.

CHANNEL 40: BACKING VOCALS 1
Insert a new track/channel and name it 'BV 1'.

Insert Fx
N/a

Sends and Returns
N/a

Panning
100 per cent left

Fader
−7.3db

Output
Master

CHANNEL 41: BACKING VOCALS 2
Insert a new track/channel and name it 'BV 2'.

Insert Fx
N/a

Sends and Returns
N/a

Panning
100 per cent right

Fader
−7.3db

Output
Master

There are no plugins directly on our backing vocal channels. However, as you'll see later we will

As per our previous backing vocals channel there are no plugins.

THE VOCAL-SECTION BUSSES

CHANNEL 42: BACKING VOCALS SUBMIX BUSS
Insert a new stereo track/channel/buss and name
it 'BV Sub'.

Insert Fx
78. Compressor
79. Channel strip
80. Multi-effects
81. De-esser 1
82. De-esser 2

Sends and Returns
N/a

Panning
Centre

Fader
+3.1db

Output
Master

This one is easier than it looks; it is a submix
destination for our separate backing vocal tracks.
The plugins are exactly the same as for our lead
vocal, but as this is a stereo buss you'll need to
insert new stereo plugins rather than just copy the
mono ones across. All the individual settings are
exactly the same though, so here they are again
in stereo!

Plugins Expanded
78. Compressor

Input	−27
Output	−18
Attack	Slow
Release	Fast
Ratio	4:1
Analogue noise	Off

Plugins Expanded
79. Channel strip

Compression	
Threshold	−12.48db
Ratio	2.4:1
Attack	82ms
Release	1
Gain reduction	−3db max

Filter	
HPF	164Hz

EQ			
−1.73db	189Hz	Bell shape	Narrow – medium Q
−1.54db	245Hz	Bell shape	Narrow – medium Q
−0.96db	305Hz	Bell shape	Narrow – medium Q
+2.30db	15kHz	Bell shape	Medium Q

80. Vocal multi-effects

Compression threshold	−18db

81. De-esser 1

Frequency	8.33kHz
Threshold	−23.8db
Attenuation	−3db max

82. De-esser 2

Frequency	2kHz
Threshold	−21.8db
Attenuation	−3db max

CHANNEL 43: VOCAL REVERB BUSS
Insert a new stereo track/channel/buss and name
it 'V Verb'.

Insert Fx
83. De-esser
84. Reverb

Sends and Returns

N/a

Panning

Centre

Fader

+2db

Output

Master

Plugins Expanded

83. De-esser

Frequency	5.2Hz
Threshold	−28db

This channel is the stereo effects buss on which we'll place our reverb of choice, but before we do, I like to insert a de-esser as my first plugin in the chain. This acts like a low-pass filter, taking off some of the spit from the signal before it hits the

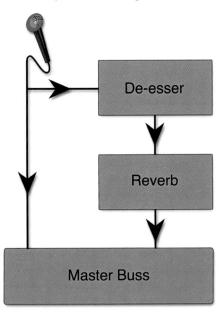

Inserting a de-esser prior to the reverb input will negate any characteristics that could potentially degrade the quality of the reverb sound.

reverb. So go ahead and insert a de-esser and dial in the settings shown.

A neat trick when sending a signal to a reverb plugin, or any other effect, is to alter the audio send in a beneficial way before the signal reaches the effect.

Plugins Expanded

84. Reverb

Reverb type	Plate
Pre-delay	150ms
Time	1.50 seconds
Size	100
Early reflections	−3db
Mix	100 per cent wet

Reverb EQ

Frequency	2.43kHz
Gain	−4.3db

I've included all the parameters that are common to most reverbs here so you can dial them in to your verb of choice. Any plate reverberation will do, just set the time and the size with the additional pre-delay and early reflections settings if your unit has them, and then just roll off that high end from 2.43kHz upwards – we don't want it overwhelming the dry lead-vocal signal. Make sure you are setting the mix to 100 per cent so that only the sound of the reverb signal is present; we can then use the channel fader to control the ratio of reverb to dry signal in the mix.

CHANNEL 44: VOCAL DELAY BUSS

Insert a new stereo track/channel/buss and name it 'V Delay'.

Insert Fx

85. Delay

Sends and Returns

N/a

Panning
Centre

Fader
−16.8db

Output
Master

Plugins Expanded
85. Delay

Decay time	*233ms
Tempo	Set to tempo of track
Delay	Eighth notes
Feedback	25 per cent
Mix	100 per cent

* I've included the decay time from my template but set this to represent an eighth note delay in milliseconds in relation to the tempo of your track.

This is identical to the delay plugin found on our instrument delay buss. The mix dial is set to 100 per cent so that only the affected sound is replayed. Set the delay time to correspond with your project tempo and you're good to go. You may recall that I use a preset called 'memory man' that appears on many delay units. It's a very grainy lo-fi delay. I don't care much for clear repeats; I like dark and moody delays that you barely notice, which are dry but wet at the same time.

THE VOCAL SECTION: ROUTING AND GROUPING

Now you've set up the vocal section and know what all the channels and busses do, it is time to action the final routing as per the following grid. Watch out for the one anomaly here: the BV Sub channel routes to the input of the Phas buss, which is located in the instrument section.

All channels go to the master buss and additional effects busses except for the backing vocals, which are deactivated from the master buss and routed to their own control buss. The backing vocal control channel then sends to the Phas channel (in addition to the master buss and V Verb) which allows us to add the classic harmonizer effect to the backing vocals.

VOCALS 65

	Master In	Vox 1	Vox 2	BV 1	BV 2	BV Sub	V Verb	V Delay	Phas
Master Out									
Vox 1	X						X	X	
Vox 2	X						X	X	
BV 1						X			
BV 2						X			
BV Sub	X						X		X
V Verb	X								
V Delay	X								

The routing grid for the vocal section.

5
THE MASTER CHANNEL

The master channel is the stereo master buss through which all sounds must pass! This is the business end of the frame for our musical picture. It all comes together here and it's important to treat it with respect. You can make or break a mix on this channel alone, so be very careful what you add here and only entertain what is most needed.

MASTER CHANNEL

Insert Fx
86. Equalizer
87. Compressor
88. Multi-effects
89. Limiter/maximizer

Sends and Returns
N/a

Panning
Centre

Fader
–10.8db

Output
Soundcard left and right outputs

Plugins Expanded
86. Equalizer

HPF	35Hz
LPF	20kHz

My first plugin is an equalizer, but you will notice I'm only using the high-pass and the low-pass filters. Any EQ or individual filters will do. All this does is clean up wasted energy on the top and bottom of the frequency spectrum. Only a finite number of bits are available, so every one you save can be used for extra headroom in the mix.

One important point to remember is that every filter has what is referred to as a slope. This is the shape that a line takes when representing the degree of gain reduction taking place across a range of frequencies. Slopes are often variable and can have a dramatic influence on the frequencies you are hearing so it is worth exploring your options and picking out the one that suits your style best.

It is not only the cut-off frequency that determines how an EQ filter will affect your audio signal but the shape of the EQ slopes too. Many

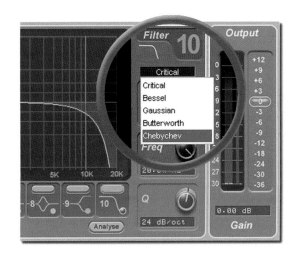

Your filter may have a way of changing the shape of its slope.

EQ plugins will have a way of changing the slope shape so choose yours carefully; pick the wrong one and you will wonder where the top end went!

Plugins Expanded
87. Compressor

Threshold	+16db
Attack	Auto
Decay time	Fastest
Compression ratio	2:1
Output	−2db
Gain reduction	−3db max

The second plugin is a buss compressor. Look for any compressor that is designed to work on combined elements that occupy a stereo buss. A ratio of 2:1 with the fastest decay time is my usual perfect setting, but a ratio of 3:1 is fun for tighter rock music or I'll go 4:1 if I'm mixing aggressively.

Regarding the attack time, the buss compressor I use has a fixed attack, which isn't a great deal of help to you. If I was to use another buss compressor, I'd shoot for a 30ms attack as a standard go-to. I know some rock producers such as Chris Lord-Alge go for a 10ms attack and use the auto release, but I personally like to let in as much attack as possible before the compressor clamps it down.

All I'm looking for this compressor to do is smooth things out by adding some buss glue and knocking back the dynamic range by 1db or so. You just want this one ticking in and out very gently.

Plugins Expanded
88. Multi-effects

Input	4.4db
Effect	35.8%
Curve	−9.4db
Output	−0.6db
Clip 0db	On
Input Split	Off

The third plugin on my master buss is another one of those all-in-one multi-effects units; the plugin increases loudness without sacrificing sonic quality or dynamic range. (See Appendix B for the manufacturer and model I use.) If you own this plugin then your goal is to make the input light tick in and out by either adjusting its input fader or the output gain from the previous plugin; I like to think of the source material 'tapping' the plugin input. If you wish to find an alternative, look for a mastering multi-effects processor that claims to do the same type of audio manipulation. It's important to find an extremely transparent model – we don't want any colour added. You can always try a demo version of the specific one I use to hear for yourself the impact it has; it will give you a sense of what I am hearing and what you need to do to match it. To be honest, this is a one-of-a-kind plugin.

Plugins Expanded
89. Limiter/maximizer

Threshold	−0.4db
Out ceiling	−0.1db
Attenuation	−1db
Quantize	16 bits
Dither	Type 1
Shaping	Normal

The final master buss plugin is a peak limiter/level maximizer. I set the output to -0.1db, which gives a little added safety against distortion on playback, and I'll pull down the threshold if I want to get a little extra volume. However, reducing the threshold squashes the dynamics in order to increase the overall volume. So only do this if absolutely necessary and be aware of the payoff between dynamics and loudness – don't push it too far. I usually like to see no more than -1db of attenuation and I'll remove this plugin altogether if the mastering is being outsourced. If I am sending my mix to a mastering engineer, obviously I'll leave the bit-reduction process to them, but if I'm providing a master file to my client then this is where I'll dither down to 16 bits.

If your peak limiter/maximizer won't dither to 16 bits you'll need to insert a dithering plugin in your final effects slot and output to a 16-bit 44.1kHz CD Industry Standard file (unless you are just concerned with HD playback).

PRE-MASTER-CHANNEL CONTROL FADER

Important: You may need to create one additional channel in order to control the level of the input signal to the master channel; please read the following to clarify:

Some DAWs will allow you to place master-channel plugins in either a pre-fader (before) or post-fader (after) position. Some will give you the choice of either. It all depends on the manufacturer. This is really important so please look inside your DAW manual if you are not sure. The plugins on your master channel must come after a post-fader so that you can use that fader to supply just the right amount of level to your mastering plugin chain. If your DAW will only insert master plugins in the pre-fader position then altering the master fader will have no effect on the feed level to the plugins as the audio has already passed them by. All is not lost in that case, however. The answer is to create one additional channel and name it 'Pre-master', then re-route everything that is presently sent to the master to this new Pre-master channel. It does nothing more than sit between your mix and the master channel and act as a control when gain staging.

To reiterate: pre-fader plugins sit before a fader; post-fader plugins are situated after a fader. The plugins on the master channel must be post-fader. This allows the master fader to control the signal level feeding the master effects. If your DAW only allows for pre-fader master plugins then a control channel must be created.

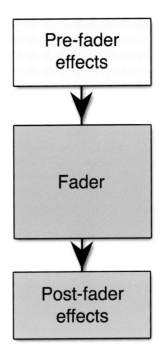

It is important to know the difference between placing your plugins in a pre-fader or post-fader position.

FINISHED TEMPLATE

Congratulations, you've set up your mix template! It is now ready to go, forevermore waiting for the next group of source tracks. Never again will you have to do all those repetitive tasks involved in starting a mix from scratch.

If you haven't already done so, now is the time to back it up to an external drive – not in another location on your computer. This template is going to save you days, weeks and months of wasted energy, give you professional consistency and catapult you straight to the business end of the mix every time, so it is good practice to store it safely.

With our template now firmly in our mind's eye and DAW, we can look at how we use a template and progress a mix through to a master recording, whilst incorporating other topics along the way.

6

IMPORTING AUDIO AND GAIN STAGING

Before we dive headfirst into a quick mix there are a couple of processes we need to address: importing and gain staging. I'm sure you will already know how to import audio; it's only attacked slightly differently within our template, but even if you've covered gain staging before you will want to stick with me on this one as I approach gain staging in a unique way. This is one very important technique that you must learn – the Deckerator gain-staging method. Remember that *without learning and applying the gain-staging method, your template will fail*. But before we get ahead of ourselves, let's look at the first task we must perform – bringing the audio into our template.

IMPORTING AUDIO

Without audio, we don't have a mix; so let's import our audio. You may have done this many times in the past or are importing for the first time. If this is new to you it's time to look in your DAW manual, but here is a brief overview leading on to how I handle the task.

Importing audio is the process of bringing the recorded tracks that reside outside of your DAW into the control of your digital workstation. It may seem a simple, obvious act, but is easy to do incorrectly. This will only become obvious when you reload a mix in the future and the files are missing or in an unknown location because they weren't imported properly. So, if you haven't

already, familiarize yourself completely with the process of moving digital files into your DAW and archiving them. Practise moving files around and watching what happens to them until you know the process inside out; this is one task you don't want to get wrong.

Whether you copy files manually into your quick-mix session folder or let your DAW handle the copying process automatically as you import, the point comes when you need to think about opening your template and importing the tracks you wish to mix. Even if you are a solo singer/songwriter creating your own source files, I would still recommend recording your tracks in a tracking session, exporting them and then re-importing them into your quick-mix template. It will pay dividends to run your song through a fresh mixing template.

However you get there, the sequence of actions to follow for importing is this:

1. Locate and open the saved template file on your computer. *Immediately select the 'save as' function* to rename the template with your chosen mix name. Save this new file in the session folder of your project. Doing this ensures the hard work and time you've spent setting up the template isn't wiped out by a single click of a mouse as you carelessly overwrite it. Get into a habit of always doing this as your first action and make sure you have a back-up in a separate location should you forget.

2. Set the sampling rate and global tempo to match the source audio you've been given or have recorded.

3. With your template open, select 'import audio' to insert the recorded parts. What I do is place them temporarily as new tracks below the final main template track. Check your DAW manual again for the best way to do this, but the outcome should be that your imported tracks are now sitting beneath your main template tracks.

4. Now lock the imported clips to the timeline, thus ensuring they can't move left or right out of sync with each other, and start dragging them one by one into their rightful place in the template above. Don't waste any time over unnecessary tasks. We don't want to rename the tracks, colour them, or insert and name any song-arrangement markers – you will get used to managing without all this superfluous information. So, for example, move a bass-guitar clip up to the bass-guitar template track and so on. We are just grabbing and moving the waveform clip. Do this for all of the imported audio clips in the project, placing them on their corresponding template tracks. You will remember for the bass drum we've got three different samples across three different

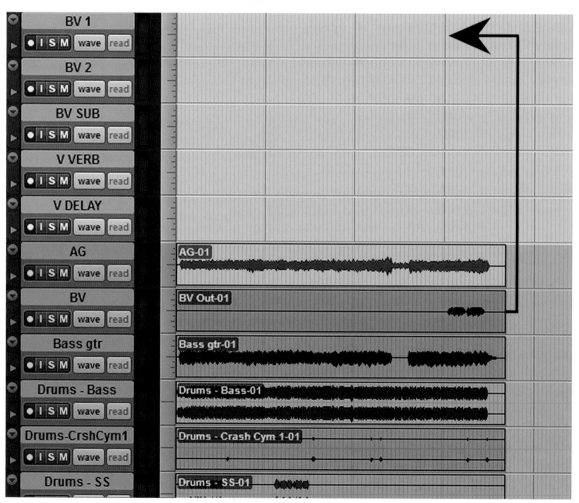

Import your source files into the empty area beneath the final track in your template and drag the waveforms into their rightful place.

tracks, so you'll want to move your bass-drum source clip into the first bass-drum track and then duplicate it two more times for the other two tracks. We want the same identical audio triggering all three bass-drum samples. The same process can be applied to the snare-drum tracks. I have pretty much covered all the standard instruments, but if you have more instances of a certain instrument in the source tracks than there are template tracks, simply duplicate the template track in question. If you have an instrument that doesn't appear on our template, then duplicate the track that shares the closest DNA to one of our template sounds – i.e. if it is a string sound duplicate and use a stringed-instrument track (guitar), or if it is a percussion instrument, copy a percussion template track (tambourine). When all the audio clips have been moved you should be left with a number of empty tracks sitting beneath your template proper. These can now be deleted.

Importing this way means no channels are renamed or corrupted and your template stays exactly as you created it.

GAIN STAGING

At the beginning of this chapter, I included the statement: *without learning and applying the gain-staging method, your template will fail*. Why will it fail? Because key to the success or failure of your template are the many compressors and limiters sprinkled all over it. It is these compressors and limiters that control the dynamics of both the individual tracks and the master channel. You will have noticed that we have entered very specific figures for each plugin threshold. This is a calculated figure, not one achieved by guesswork or plucked out of the air. These threshold levels have purpose, always remain constant, and need to be fed just the right level of input signal to make your template dance. Too much level and you will kill it; too little and it will be out of control.

So, with all the source files now in their proper location, our next task is to set the gain of each clip so that all the instruments are sending the correct input levels to the individual processors that will control their dynamic.

This task is achieved visually, so you can do this quickly (without playing the song) merely by using your eyes. The tool we need to do this is, you've guessed it, our clip-gain tool. The clip-gain tool increases or decreases the playback level of each clip at source before it enters the channel and plugin chain, so it is the perfect tool to use to set the optimum level to feed our hungry plugins (jump to the DAW manual if you don't know where it is or what it does). Use the clip-gain tool to nudge the waveform's gain up or down until the average energy of the clip occupies 50 per cent of the given area, i.e. a quarter of empty space above and a quarter of empty space below. It's as simple as that. It will never overload this way. Do this for each clip and we're good to go.

We are working on the average level here so expect transient spikes to encroach into the upper 50 per cent. It is these brief peaks of audio that we want to affect with our processors. The black horizontal line you see here represents the threshold level for the compressors and limiters.

Here is where setting specific threshold levels for all our compressors and limiters now pays off, because by altering the audio clip's gain to fill 50 per cent of the allotted area, each instrument should now be 'kissing' the first processor at just the right level. By kissing I mean that, at its loudest point, a signal should just push through the threshold, resulting in no more than 3db of gain reduction. This amount of gain reduction is all that's required. If you think about it, that's up to 3db off the peaks of one sound because of one individual processor. With all our other compressors and limiters clicking in and out, that adds up to some serious overall multi-layered dynamic control, subtle manipulation that is applied in such a way that no one unit is doing so much that it kills the sound, and yet we're still letting the music shine through.

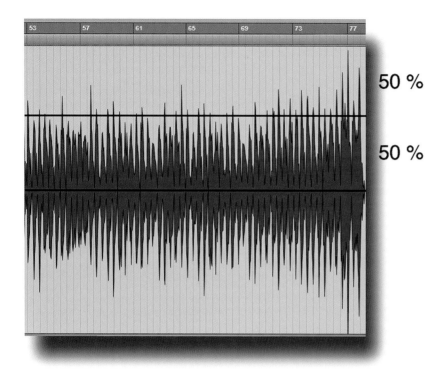

Use the clip gain tool so that the average energy of your waveform fills approximately 50 per cent of your audio track.

50 %

50 %

Until you are completely confident with the correct position of your visual clip gain, you should check the signal is flowing as it should be by calling up each plugin and looking for the right amount of kissing being applied. If, for whatever reason, it's not happening, just readjust the visual clip form until it does. Don't be tempted to change the threshold level; this must always remain the same. Practice makes perfect and you will soon get used to seeing the right level of gain instantly every time, until you no longer need to check – you'll just know.

I often say I could mix a song just by looking at it, and I'm only half joking! When you've got this spot on with practice, you'll see that everything falls into place and you are 80 per cent there within minutes.

You may have to do a little chopping and changing of the gain envelope of source files that are wildly out of control. It is not unusual to be given a track that varies from quiet to loud from one section to another, or measure by measure as the track progresses. This can represent the natural progression of a performance in line with all the other musical voices and can be a wonderful thing if intentional, but often it is the result of lack of control from the performer or because various different takes have been compiled into one easy-to-manage track. Either way, check to see how the part interacts with the song as a whole. If the level swings are unintentional, simply split the loudest and softest parts and adjust the clip gain of each separated section so that a more consistent level is achieved throughout. Then shift the complete track as a whole up or down to match the 50 per cent rule discussed previously.

When it comes to gain staging the master-channel plugin chain, it is vitally important to hit the master plugins with just the right amount of input level. Too much and you will over-compress and squash the life out of your mix, but too little and the master plugins become ineffective. With all those optimized tracks hitting red in the mix, things can get a little heated when it comes to the master channel – did I mention that I like to mix hot? You can get away with a few red lights in the mix thanks to the headroom afforded by 24 bits or more, but there should be no red lights on the master channel, please.

So how do we supply just the right amount of input feed through the master channel without having a visual waveform to aid us? Well the burden lies on the common fader; just raise or lower the fader until the optimum level is reached. You can either measure the correct level using a VU meter or simply call up the first buss compressor and alter the control fader until -1db of attenuation is showing on the loudest parts of the song. If your chain is set up correctly this should translate to -1db of gain reduction on the final limiter/maximizer too.

You will need to constantly check that the level of the input feed into the master channel isn't getting too hot or too cold. I am forever checking and moving my master fader up or down to compensate. It is really important as it affects what you are hearing in the mix and how you will react.

7
MIXING

As I mentioned at the start of this book, it was never my intention to rewrite the book on mixing, but rather to share my secrets with you and show you how I mix. I want to give you specific information on how to set up your DAW so that it is a super-quick mixing machine like mine. This chapter follows that theme. It contains everything you need to know to balance your quick mix to a professional standard and get your template rocking. This could be all you'll ever need to know or you may choose to delve into the science of mixing further. Whatever path you choose, always try to be the best you can possibly be. Don't settle for second best; mixing fast shouldn't mean a lessening of quality and every time you sit down to mix generate a positive vibe. Think to yourself, 'I am going to nail this mix'. So much of mixing is down to attitude. Own your mixing desk and all that flows through it, follow this guide and with a little practice and critical listening you'll soon be outputting high-quality, pro-sounding mixes too.

STARTING A MIX

By now, you have set up your template, imported your audio, dragged the waveforms into your template tracks and set your levels visually using the Deckerator gain-staging method. What next? How do you now go about creating a pro-sounding quick mix?

Well, to start with let's press play. It may surprise you to hear how close you are to a final mix already. There have been occasions when simply dragging in my audio has been enough! More often than not

though, there will be some re-balancing of levels and sweetening of EQ to do. I figure my template will get me 80 per cent of the way there. Think about that, that's an 80 per cent time-saving on every mix you do. No need to reinvent the wheel every time and no need to do the same repetitive tasks that you know are always going to be the same on every mix you do.

Bear in mind that if this is your first running of the template there may be some remedial gain staging of the plugin chains to do. This is normal and a one-off process. Work through it and save your changes as your new template master – be assured that this is the framework for success.

So, you've given the song a listen, what now? Well it might surprise you to know that one simple thought goes through my mind on every mix I start, and that is: 'Am I going to be aggressive or mild?' I keep my choices narrowed down to these two; it makes mixing easier.

Hold that thought in your mind, give the song another play and ask yourself 'Does the song want an aggressive or mild mix?' Let the music and your instincts tell you.

I will clarify what I mean by being aggressive or mild, and how to achieve a difference. It's all down to the amount of compression I add on the mix and master channels. The EQ will always stay the same, but switching the compressor's ratio from 2:1 to 3:1 or 4:1 results in a more aggressive mix. I can also hit the thresholds harder, thus applying more gain reduction which will be perceived as being more aggressive too.

The following diagram shows an example of how switching the compression ratio of a mix

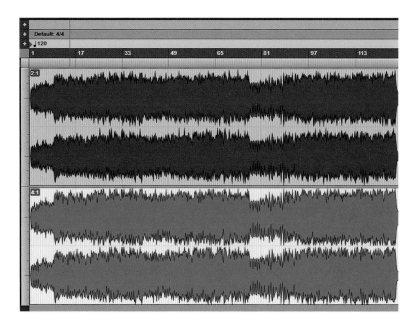

The first waveform is mixed through the standard template with compression of 2:1; the second waveform is a more aggressive 4:1 setting.

bass and the individual instruments, finishing with the vocal, basically following the layout of the mixing console left to right. Listen carefully to each sound as you un-mute it and don't always assume it is broken and needs fixing. Sometimes what you have is perfect already and doing nothing is the right decision for the mix.

reduces the dynamic range. The top waveform (2:1) shows a mix with 12db of dynamic range, whilst the lower waveform (4:1) has a dynamic range of 10db. Louder mixes with less dynamics are perceived as more aggressive.

Try it for yourself so you can see and hear the difference. Export a mixed stereo file with all the compressor ratios set to the template defaults – this is a mild template we've set up. Then do nothing else except switch all the ratios up a notch, i.e. from 2:1 to 3:1 or 4:1 and then export a second stereo file. When comparing the two (assuming you are hitting the compressors correctly) you will see and hear that the second mix is more squashed (compressed) which will be perceived as more aggressive by the listener. Make this your first decision: aggressive or mild?

Now we need to balance our mix with subtle fader level and EQ corrections. How you do this will ultimately be down to your own musical preferences and the choices you make, but certain workflow practices remain constant.

Always follow the same path through your mix. Repetition is the key to success. Start by muting all the channels and then bring them back in one at a time, correcting each one until you are happy it fits your vision. Drums are first, then add the

For the pesky sounds that don't fall into your lap and need help to shine, work quickly and instinctively. You will be constantly changing and re-balancing as you go so don't stress over small details at this stage. The level you set initially will rarely be the finishing level for the track. Your movements will become finer and finer as you progress until any move you make upsets the correct balance.

EQUALIZE AND BALANCE SOUND

The way I recommend you approach a mix, and the way I approach one, is to pretend you are painting a picture. The space between the speakers represents your canvas. You'll want to ensure both you and the admiring onlookers are able to see every detail that you paint within your finished masterpiece. For example, if you paint a man sitting on a bench in a park you can clearly see that man on the bench.

If you then decide to paint a huge skyscraper in front of him you can no longer see your central figure, just the skyscraper.

It is the same with sound. We call it masking.

Certain sounds will mask other sounds and it is not as straightforward as you may initially think. There are psychoacoustic factors that come into play that are way beyond the brief of this book. Just be aware that masking is happening and always work to free a sound from its mask. To do that you need to move your sounds up, down, left or right or do some kind of three-dimensional shading as you would with a painting so everything can be seen by the ears.

Mixing is similar to painting; try to define each instrument so that the whole composition is clear for all to see. *Created from images by Mabel Amber, Pixabay and Wener Weisser, Pixabay.*

Instruments can easily become hidden by other larger sounding instruments. *Created from images by Mabel Amber, Pixabay; Wener Weisser, Pixabay; and Maitelli, Pixabay.*

Continuing with the painting analogy, an artist designs a fake three-dimensional picture by fooling the eye, and subsequently the brain, into thinking that what lies before them on a flat canvas is indeed a real 3D image. They do this with shadowing, perspective and contrast between light and dark. By presenting the brain with rules that it knows to be true in the real world, the illusion is created.

If we now apply that to music and our mix, we can see that we too create a fake image. The spread of a stereo sound-field appears to the listener to be coming from all areas between the left and the right speaker, yet we know this to be false. Sound is only coming from one left speaker and one right speaker. However, the brain is fooled into thinking that centrally panned instruments sit right in front of the listener. How? Because the brain has learned from real-world situations that if an identical sound wave reaches each ear at the same time, with the same level of energy and frequency response, then the only possible place for that sound is directly in front of the listener.

We know this as the phantom image. If the sound source was positioned off to the left, the left ear would hear it sooner than the right ear and the brain would know the source is to the left; off to the right and the right ear will hear it sooner and the brain will interpret the signal as being to the right.

Another life rule that the brain knows, which can help us deceive it, is that high-end frequencies lessen over distance travelled. So we can roll off the top end of a sound and the brain will perceive it as further back in the mix. Or conversely, we can brighten a sound up to help bring it to the front.

So, we can move sounds left or right, up or down and back to front. Left to right movement is achieved by panning, EQ is used for up and down, and a combination of volume levels, reverb spaces and delays are used for added depth front to back. Never cover anything up, keep it visible within the picture frame of the speakers and move sound around until you can hear it or it pokes out! It's literally as easy as that. That and practice.

So, paint a sonic landscape and fill it with interesting elements that are clear to see with the mind's eye. Highlight the most important features with additional care and attention to elevate them from the background melee and use a base wash of reverb and delays to fill the gaps.

Think of your studio monitors as the boundaries that form the framework for your musical work of art.

Of course, it is possible to step outside of the picture frame too by using stereo widening tools, but be careful as the effects they create will disappear in mono.

Having established that we need to move sounds around, it might surprise you to know that nearly all the moves you will make come down to two factors: changes in sound level or movements in time. Some changes in level are obvious. You raise a channel's fader and the loudness increases. But panning is a change in level too – a change in level between the left and right channels. EQ also works by changing the level of the frequencies you've selected. Compressors and limiters, too, work by altering level, whereas reverbs, echo delays, chorus pedals and flange effects, for example, all work by shifting a copy of the sound in time.

Don't become weighed down with all the possibilities though. Remember, we have already made 80 per cent of our decisions on our mix within our template! We've already set our compressors and limiters to control the individual elements and overall dynamics; we've already set our parallel compression to add punch to the drums; we've already set our go-to EQ curves; we've already set our delays, reverbs and doubling effects; we've already built our plugin chains on all channels and optimized the gain staging and we've already got our killer vocal sound. So, we can now sit back with a smile and listen to our overall mix in the knowledge that just subtle balancing and a touch of EQ correction to taste is all we need.

So how do you know when and how to make positive changes for the better? For me it is a feeling, I just know. This may not sound very helpful upon first reading until we look at how I've progressed to the stage where I am able to work on instinct and feeling, without too much thinking. I wasn't born with an ability to mix. I've done my time learning my craft through accredited, formal sound-technology courses and through my own exploration of this wonderful medium. That's where the feeling comes from, that's where the instinct is honed, through practice, practising some more and then some!

I've included an exercise you can do to train your ears to recognize the full range of the frequency spectrum and how it affects certain sounds. You can find it later in this chapter. Learn all the frequencies. Frequencies will never change; once learned they will work for you for life. The low end always lives in a certain space, always has done and always will. Acoustic guitar always plays nicely within a certain frequency range and it is the same with voices and pianos, etc.; any sound you can think of has its own set of frequencies that are pleasing and not so pleasing. This will never change. They are the fundamentals and harmonics that make a guitar sound like a guitar or a flute sound like a flute. Make it your goal to learn them. That is what I did. I looked at all the frequencies on paper and matched them to my ear. I found where each instrument lives within the frequency spectrum and what range it goes up or down to, and now it has become second nature for me.

Mixing takes practice just like anything else so make a habit of practising every day and view it as a journey through an ever-changing landscape of knowledge to be absorbed. Learn something new every day.

One last thought on the masking effect we spoke of earlier: don't assume that a sound you think needs changing is where the actual problem lies. The cause can often be found within a sound that is creating the masking effect, so make it a habit to mute the other instruments that may be clashing with the sound you are focused on to check. View the mute button as your friend and the solo button as an enemy, to be avoided at all costs.

It will help you to learn and progress as a mixer by analyzing commercial CDs of other mixers' work. Take notes on the choices they've made regarding panning, EQ and levels together with the processing they've applied. What effects have they used? Do they have a special production trick they use on every mix they do that gives them their sound? Don't be afraid to emulate others,

take a bit here and a bit there and make them your own. It's often said there is nothing new under the sun. Likewise, there is nothing new in mixing – just talented minds that use what we all have in a unique and inventive way.

Apart from your ears and mind's eye there are additional tools that can help you balance your sounds and learn the frequency spectrum of instruments, the main one being a spectrum analyzer. Most spectrum analyzers have the ability to give an accurate, real-time visual representation of the frequencies present in an instrument or group of instruments, and can also show your audio stereo positioning, frequency spread and peak/RMS levels too.

When making any sound-shaping decisions or reference mixing there is one important phenomenon to be aware of, and that is that any instrument will sound better the louder it is. Louder is perceived as better. This means that if you do nothing to a sound except turn it up you will think it is a better version than before. This is very important. Make sure you are improving a sound and not just thinking you are improving it by making it louder. It is a smoke-and-mirrors trick used by many plugin designers to wow the listener. The answer is to always level match the before and after version. The level of the signal entering a plugin should be the same as the level exiting the plugin – you can use a meter to check.

THE FREQUENCY SPECTRUM AND EAR TRAINING

In the previous section we touched on the idea that the frequency spectrum never changes, and that it will benefit you to learn the frequency spectrum and how individual frequencies affect individual instruments. I am, therefore, presenting the frequency spectrum as I see it and showing an easy, repetitive exercise you can use to internalize them. It's worth noting that there are differing ideas as to how to split the full frequency spectrum up and how to label the respective zones, so don't be surprised to see them represented differently elsewhere.

THE FREQUENCY SPECTRUM

The frequency spectrum can be thought of as a way of documenting the full range of human hearing from the upper to the lower limits.

It is worth noting though that not everyone hears every frequency. How high or low one person can hear depends on each individual. The frequency spectrum is measured in hertz (Hz) and kilohertz (kHz). 1,000Hz = 1kHz. It can also be expressed musically in octave bands. Each octave equals a doubling or halving of the previous octave depending on whether the scale is rising or declining.

HOW TO TRAIN THE EAR

This is a very simple exercise. I recommend you practice for ten to fifteen minutes a day, making it part of your daily routine. It's a good one to start your session with as the frequencies will stay with you during the mix.

Firstly, choose your instrument to work on and then insert an EQ plugin into the relevant channel.

If you can, choose an EQ with dial knobs rather than one long continuous display as it's easier to visualize the musical zones around a circular knob. So, with an EQ inserted it is as easy as playing back the source file, boosting or cutting the EQ gain (whichever you are practising), and slowly sweeping through each section back and forth, one at a time.

Two exercises to practise

1. Listening – really listen to the instrument and internalize how the sound is affected by each frequency boost and cut. It is vitally important to know when a sound is lacking in certain frequencies or has too much of others. You can do this on complete mixes too for mastering purposes.

2. Moving around the spectrum – spend time jumping around the spectrum via the different dials and zones as if you were learning where the notes are on an instrument. Think of a frequency number and the musical zone in which it lives and then try to go straight to that frequency. Make it your goal to be able to instantly jump to any one frequency and know where it lies regarding musical regions, i.e. bass, mid, presence, etc.

DEFINING THE MIX

MIX VISUALIZATION

It may interest you to know that I see the frequency spectrum as a set of colours. This is a phenomenon called 'synesthesia', something that I have always experienced. Synesthesia is not a condition that is limited to music but can be triggered by other things such as numbers and dates. However, many famous musicians and sound engineers

16K Octave 10: Upper highs

| **8K** Octave 9: Treble |

4K Octave 8: Edge presence range

| **2K** Octave 7: Upper mid-range |

1K Octave 6: Mid-range

| **500 Hz** Octave 5: Lower mid-range |

250 Hz Octave 4: Mud-range thickness

| **125 Hz** Octave 3: Upper bass warmth |

62.50 Hz Octave 2: Lower bass

| **31.25 Hz** Octave 1: Bottom end rumble |

The Frequency Spectrum divided into Hertz and musical octaves.

have this condition, so if you interpret sound in any unusual way, go with it, it may be your key to a fresh new sound. How do you see it? Do you see it at all? It's not unusual to not have any visual representation of sound at all but if you can 'see' sound as well, it helps. Even if you don't see sound visually but have a good imagination you can still teach the brain to recognize sound by forming a picture in your mind of how you wish to see music. This will become more concrete over time as the brain learns how to see frequencies and will help you when shaping your mix.

I've always found it helps to use descriptive words that express clearly what you are feeling or what you want to feel. Try to be as descriptive as you possibly can. This will help you as you sculpt sounds into the form you need for clarity in your mix, and will also help you get your vision across to collaborators and fellow audiophiles. As an example, if I said, 'The lead female vocal has too much 2k', you'd understand what I was saying (that the female vocal has an exaggerated boost within the 2kHz frequency range) but it wouldn't mean much to you. But if I say, 'Man that female vox is harsh and has way too much 2k. It's like you're taking a butter knife and jabbing it into my forehead!' you know exactly what I'm saying and feeling, right? You've been there and felt the pain!

The best tool to help with visualizing a mix is again the good old spectrum analyzer. I use them all the time. I feel it's very helpful to actually look at the frequency spectrum through an analyzer and be able to see what I am hearing.

Mix Concept

Regarding the overall concept of a song and mix, you can get in too deep when you go digging around, looking for unnecessary distractions. We are not trying to put men or women on the moon; we are just trying to put them on the radio. It's not rocket science so don't complicate it. Whether you are working for clients or mixing your own music the key is consistency; this is what will bring you repeat work or repeat plays. Keep it simple and repeat what works, i.e. your template.

Synesthesia is a phenomenon whereby a person hears or sees something that results in them visualizing a colour.

I consider my job to be taking what the client or artist gives me, the bare bones of their creation, and making it sound the very best it can, according to their vision. I will always ask my client or artist what their vision is and work to it, but I never look at lyrics. I don't care what they are saying; it would be like asking the guitar player for their tablature! Sound is sound is sound. Blend it to a vision, no more than that.

The Perfect Mix Misconception

Let's be clear on this; here is one statement that I am sure all mix engineers, producers, musicians and creatives will concur with – there is no such thing as perfection. Please don't stress yourself trying to achieve it. Perfection is a moving target that keeps on disappearing out of reach. You may struggle endlessly to achieve what you perceive as perfection, but cracks will soon appear upon greater inspection and new benchmarks will be set. With continued dedication, application and practice you will, without doubt, reach a level of professionalism and a quality of output that matches commercial CDs. You will only know this by looking back one day. To me this is as good as it gets. The closest I will get to a perfect mix is one where I listen back years later and go, 'Damn, I did that?'

But even then, you will still listen to other mixers and prefer aspects of their work to yours, be filled with self-doubt and think you've still got a long way to go. I still do that now! Be aware of the doubting voice in your head and accept that it's just part of our make-up as humans. I think it's what drives us on to higher achievements. Don't ever give up on your journey of personal evolution.

VOLUME AND PANNING

RIDING FADERS

If you have been used to riding faders within your mix or you are just learning the rules, you may have read or heard that to breathe life into a mix or to get certain parts to stand out you need to ride the fader. There is software available to do exactly that. You may have read that to get a vocal to stand out, you must ride up the start of each word in order to catch the initial syllable for increased intelligibility.

All that may indeed be true, but this may come as a surprise to you: I do little if any riding of faders! I like to let the music ride itself. Yes, I'll ride up certain sections – the chorus, bridges or lead solo, for example, but for the most part the way I mix means parts level themselves out. You'll see this for yourself as you play with our template, how everything becomes levelled out because of the way we've set ourselves up.

I use a lot of limiters and compressors, but with very little compression from each one. Remember, a compressor or limiter is doing the same thing as your finger on a fader. The result is many imaginary fingers riding all these little faders within our compressors and limiters so we don't have to. Trust the process, trust the template and have the courage to leave the faders alone.

LEFT-CENTRE-RIGHT (L-C-R) PANNING

Panning can be described as the spread of mono-sound signals within a stereo sound-field, i.e. the moving of instruments left or right within the stereo image that appears between the speakers. It is actually achieved by altering the ratio of volume between the left and right channels. An increased level in the left channel moves the sound to the left, while an increase in level to the right channel moves a sound to the right. Therefore, panning an instrument fully left within the stereo sound-field means that music is coming from the left monitor only; volume in the right monitor is reduced to nothing. Pan fully right and only the right monitor is active. The centre-panned position is achieved

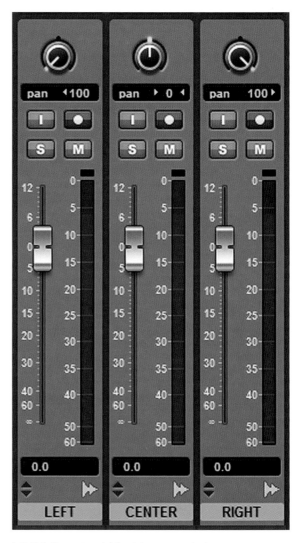

L-C-R (left, centre, right) mixing uses only three pan positions.

when both the left and right channels carry identical signals – this is referred to as the phantom image.

How you pan your sounds will come down to your own personal preferences. Do you know what your preferences are right now? Make a point of finding out; do some research on your favourite bands, artists and mixes. What panning protocol do they follow? You may be surprised to find that one style is prominent or that it varies and is inconclusive. Some mix engineers won't pan anything further than half left and half right while others swear by L-C-R panning which is the practice of only using three pan positions – far left, far right and centre. L-C-R panning follows a system that was established back in the 1960s as recording studios made the transition from mono to stereo recordings. The mixing consoles at the time didn't have panning as we know it today, but instead used a method of sending signals to the left, right, and centre group or master busses.

You will note from the panning we have already set up in our template that I prefer L-C-R for the most part. I like to throw sounds out as wide as possible. I pan hard left, hard right and down the middle and let the reverbs and delays fill in the spaces. I have never heard a mix that is too wide and, of course, adding stereo effects pulls the sounds across the stereo sound-field, blending everything together in a pleasing way. The only exception to this rule is where I will have fills played on a fiddle or steel guitar, which I will set to half left and half right respectively. I recommend you do the same.

HARDWARE

MONITOR LEVELS AND REPLAY SYSTEMS
It is worth thinking for a moment about replay levels and different systems because they too are a very important link in your hit-making chain. There is a great deal of information on this subject freely available, and again it's outside of the scope of this book as it is not my intention to repeat common

knowledge but to present my individual take on mixing. There are, however, a couple of important aspects that I feel I ought to mention.

The level you set your monitor gain to will influence what you are hearing and subsequently what you mix. There is an optimum playback level at which the human ear perceives all frequencies at their flattest. This occurs between 80–90db (83db is normally quoted). This is obviously a great level to start hearing your mix. We are talking about the sound-pressure level at the point of delivery when the music hits your ears as it springs forth from the monitors (you will need an SPL meter to measure this accurately). However, you may wish to vary your monitor level as you mix as different levels accentuate different important aspects of your mix. Experiment and listen for yourself.

Personally, I am always going up and down in volume. Some days I mix louder than others. I have no set rules ever, but then I have been doing this gig for a long time and know my monitors, how my room responds and how that will transfer to a balanced mix. The last phrase, 'transfers to a balanced mix', is key. In the end, this is all that matters. You must know how what you do inside your mix environment affects the results that are heard in the outside world and playback levels and monitors play a big part in this. The process of trial and error is the only way forward, so get experimenting and writing down how the changes you make alter what you hear when you play your mixes out.

I always check my mixes in the studio (via my main monitors and a boombox), the car and through earbuds. Not only am I checking how my own mix has travelled but also how it compares to other mixes. I will be listening to my mix to make sure it comes up to my standards and then I will compare it against other commercial mixes to check it's in line with theirs.

Regarding the monitor systems I use in my studio, I have two different sets of monitors, which I switch between. I run a pair of Mackie HR824 Mk2 with a Quested 18 subwoofer and a pair of Wathen Reference .5 monitors with matching subwoofer.

My trusty old boombox.

I also run a feed from my mixing desk to an old boombox that I've had for seventeen years! I like to switch to this when my ears have gotten just a little too used to the sound of my main monitors; it gives me a fresh perspective and allows me to hear what my mix sounds like on a trashy system. It was the cheapest one I could find that had an auxiliary input!

You will find for yourself a set of monitors that suits your ears and style. You may have to try a few before you find a set you are comfortable with, or you may not have that luxury and will have to work with what you have. Don't see this as a negative. If you don't have the means to be able to afford the monitors you would like, remember all that matters is that your mixes travel well, that they play back the best they can on as many playback systems as possible. Many great songs have been mixed on all types of monitors – it's in the ears not the gear. If you are able, though, I'd recommend hooking up at least one additional set of monitors and switching during mixing. This along with referencing commercial CDs will ensure you keep perspective.

THE BENEFITS OF MONO

When I first started mixing back in the day it was mandatory to check your mixes in mono as a lot of radio stations broadcasted in mono only. If you are not aware of the differences between mono and stereo, now is the time to reach for your DAW manual. Both mono and stereo mixing have a colourful history that is well worth taking a look through in your downtime.

Nowadays everything is stereo, but you may be surprised to learn that mono still has a big part to play both as a balancing tool and as a means of adding impact to a mix. Creatively, a mono mix can be a powerhouse of a mix without the distractions of stereo's bells and whistles. Mono mixing is in fact harder to pull off as there is no panning available to move sounds to the side out of the way. Every decision is based on a top-to-bottom stacking system so a lot of care must be taken to make sure instruments are heard.

Try a mix in mono to see what I mean – a true mono mix, not a centre-panned balance with stereo reverb and delays, return all reverbs and effects in mono too so you'd better add some pre-delay on those verbs to stop them swamping your sounds!

In reality, you will never do a true mono mix these days. The closest you will come will probably be a stagnant centrally panned mix with stereo reverbs and delays for added stereo imagery to enhance the musical beauty that the stereo sound-field can impart. Or perhaps you might create a pseudo-mono balanced verse (everything panned centrally) that blooms into a wide stereo-rich chorus that can create a beautiful lifting sensation in a song and give the listener a powerful hit. Even then a lot of the cool effects you hear on today's stereo mixes that optimize the stereo format collapse and disappear when played back in mono, so it's still worth switching the mono button on to see how much of your mix disappears, even if it's more out of curiosity than necessity.

I still do a lot of mixing in mono. I use it as a balancing tool and suggest you do the same. Listening in mono when you start a mix will give you an awesome foundation on which to build your mix as it gives you a better idea as to the relationship between your kick, snare and bass guitar – all these centrally panned rhythmic instruments that we bring in first to get the rhythm section rocking.

It will also serve you well to think of every mix as a combination of mono and stereo, often referred to as 'mid and side' where mid is the left + right (mono) and sides are left – right (the stereo field). There are many plugins now that use 'mid/side' manipulation and this too can be used as a great analysis tool as well as creatively.

REFERENCE MIXING

To this day, I still listen and compare my work to other mix engineers, which is often referred to as reference mixing. I feel strongly that you should do the same. There are some awesome plugins that handle everything for you. If you're going to compare two mixes via a manual set-up it is vital that you ensure each mix plays back through the same output medium at exactly the same level, as an increase or decrease of volume alters the frequency response that we hear (of course, the commercial mix needs to bypass your master chain).

I put every mix I do up against the competition. I try to mimic what I like in other people's work, weaving it into my own mixes in my own way. I like to look at other mixes through a frequency analyzer to see what the difference is between mine and theirs. I've even gone as far as to EQ match my mix to theirs or morph it into mine by blending the two. I often do this to see if it helps or hurts my mix. If it makes it worse, I ditch it; if it makes it better, then why not? Don't discount anything until you have tried it for yourself.

If you are not familiar with EQ matching software, the plugin in question analyzes the frequency response (EQ curve) of two different mixes, first a source (a commercial CD) and then a target (your mix). The plugin then renders the EQ curve of the

source onto the target mix. Basically, your mix gets equalized the same way as the commercial reference mix. Many people discount this by saying, 'All mixes are different; each has distinct tones and balances. How can that possibly work?' Forget all that. It's as simple as this: does it make your mix better or worse?

PRIMARY AREAS OF ANY MIX

THE LOW END

There are a couple of key areas that will make or break your mix: the low end or crucial bass frequencies, and the lead vocal. You'll know yourself the importance of these by the amount of real estate they take up on chat forums and blogs. That is not to lessen the importance of every other aspect of your mix. A successful mix is one made up of many small decisions across all instruments and arrangements that add up to a whole, but these two will stick out more than the rest and listeners will know when you've got it wrong.

The way I handle those all-important bass frequencies is this:

1. Hi-pass the bass guitar at around 80Hz.
2. Fill in 60–80Hz with the bass drum.
3. Pad out sub 60Hz with a bass-enhancer plugin on the bass guitar.
4. Hi-pass the master buss to around 30–35Hz.

So, what's going on here? Well, I've found that hi-passing the bass guitar sits it right on top of the bass drum, which is normally boosted at 60Hz. I then back-fill the sub 60Hz space with a bass-enhancer plugin on the bass-guitar channel. This works best for me. I'm always looking to clean up the low end and take out the unwanted frequencies that just produce mud and don't sound pleasing. This method gives me control over the lower frequency bands. I always sit a bass guitar on top of a bass drum without exception, and using a bass-enhancing plugin will help get a great bass sound on smaller speakers. The technology it uses is based on psychoacoustics, and it actually generates synthetic frequencies that fool the brain into thinking the missing frequencies that small speakers are unable to generate are actually present.

Of course, it still comes down to the judgement and instinct that I have built over many years – knowing when too much is too much, knowing when there is something missing or when to nudge a fader just a touch more to get the bass guitar and bass drum bouncing. But you too will forge your own magical powers over time.

The tips and tricks that I've laid out in this chapter hold true for these key areas too, not just a full mix. Make use of commercial references and analyzers to see as well as hear what everyone else is doing. The whole point of this book is to show you the immense power of template mixing. You can see that having already set up our template and made 80 per cent of our decisions we are immediately free to focus on these key areas that make a difference. Rather than spend an hour equalizing a bass drum (we've already done that), we can ask where it sits correctly and balance it in seconds.

VOCALS

The human voice is an incredible instrument with

Lead and backing vocals should be prominent within your mix.

an infinitely diverse range of sounds. Complete arrangements of complex songs can be built up by using only the voice box and some air. Every voice is unique and can only be captured by a microphone. The type and brand of microphone, together with the ability of the performer, will have a massive impact on the recorded results and if your mixed vocal does not sound natural to the listener then the mix is compromised.

The lead vocal is *the* most important part of every mix without exception. It has to sound right. Every potential listener hears the human voice almost constantly every day within all imaginable environments. Whatever the voice, whatever the acoustic space, they will have heard it. They also have a lifetime of listening to a recorded voice too and will have an in-built sensor for knowing what a recorded vocal should sound like. It's important to know that the human voice heard in a natural environment is not necessarily the same as a voice heard through a recorded medium. The important message here is that the lead vocal leaping out from our template should be exactly as the listener expects to hear it within a specific genre. Let's reiterate these points as they are so important. You need to be aware of exactly what makes a recorded vocal sound right, and also be aware that the genre that a musical creation falls within will influence the production values it is given.

Here is where you can afford a little smile to yourself and thank the wonder of template mixing because we have already addressed 80 per cent of these concerns, but that does not mean you shouldn't be aware of what's going on; it is important to dissect and know.

Within our template we have already crafted a vocal sound that has all the ingredients of a great recorded vocal. We have balanced the vocal performance with manual clip-gain editing and then with different levels of light compression, each smoothing out the loudest parts. We have equalized the vocal in a pleasing way by removing the unwanted muddy frequencies and enhancing the air and brightness, making it shine. We have finally added two levels of de-essing to de-ess and de-honk the voice.

As with all aspects of musical arrangements, performance, sound engineering, music technology, mixing and mastering, there are many ways to achieve the same goal. There is no right or wrong, just different styles and ideals. Mixing a vocal is no different. Many mix engineers will throw the vocal sound in early on in the mix, usually after the drums and bass, stating that they feel it is better to build the instruments around the vocal so the vocal has its own space in the mix. Great if that works for them, but I've spent an age trying to sit the vocal right; I have tried all different approaches and I've settled on a technique that works for me and is as follows.

You will see in our template that we have created two lead-vocal channels. This is the secret; one is an exact copy of the other. Both are identical in every way and must always remain so. Anything you do to one channel you must replicate on the other. So, if you change a parameter within a plugin on one channel, copy it to the other and so on. I spent many years trying to get the vocal to sit right on top of the backing track and this works for me every time. It is the technique, combined with the vocal plugin chain that I haven't changed for over ten years, that is the reason they call me 'the vocal guy' in Nashville and why labels dial me up when they want an upfront, radio-friendly vocal.

There is an easy way to check both vocal channels are identical during your mix: with all auxiliary-effect sends muted, invert the polarity and switch on one channel only. If both channels are identical in every way then both vocals will cancel each other out and the lead vocal will magically disappear. If you still hear any remnants of the vocal, then something is different between the two channels.

And again, as with the low-end section, the previous tips and tricks can help. Make use of commercial references, compare your vocal with others to see what everyone else is doing and get a feel for where it sits right. Before too long, you will just know.

DOUBLE-TRACKED VOCALS

To avoid any misunderstanding, it's worth taking a moment to differentiate between a double-tracked vocal and the two channels of vocals within our template.

The two channels within our template, as we have learned already, are merely one lead-vocal performance and plugin chain that has been replicated a second time, by way of a second channel that is an exact copy of the first.

This is totally different to the practice of double-tracking a vocal. Double-tracking a vocal is achieved by asking the vocalist to perform a second take of the lead-vocal part. The vocalist must try to match the second performance as closely as is humanly possible to the first. If executed properly, the listener should not be able to notice there are two separate voices; they should appear as one as any difference will act as a distraction. The result is a thickened vocal. There are various plugins that claim to be able to automatically recreate a double-tracked vocal, and indeed they have their own sound if this is what you are after, but there is no substitute for a real double-tracked vocal.

Having said that, personally, I never double-track vocals. Nobody in Nashville or country music in general does, it's more a pop trick. But if the genre of music you are mixing necessitates a double-tracked vocal track then go ahead and duplicate the two existing vocal channels, call them 'Vox Dbl' and handle the pair in exactly the same way – i.e. ensure that both double-tracked vocal channels are exactly the same.

ANALOGUE EMULATIONS

Analogue versus digital: the battle of the sound-recording and mixing formats! So much has been written over the years on the subject that I'm not sure I can add anything except to tell you of my experience and thoughts.

I switched to the digital world of Pro Tools many years ago when it became apparent to me that so much time could be saved through the use of instant recall and templates. To me this was a game-changer, and I've never looked back. It was very important to me personally to work as quickly and as efficiently as possible. You may have different values or hear artefacts within the digital realm that I don't. I only use digital in-the-box technology. Nothing analogue exists in my mixing world. I even use digital reverbs because of the ability to save and recall patches.

Should we try to emulate the analogue past digitally through analogue emulation? For me, it's a big no. Don't get me wrong, I've tried all the tools but for me all they do is add back the noise and hiss that I've been working hard trying to remove. It's just not my thing. I like a clean, bright, upfront sound with all the trash taken away.

THE MENTAL DEMANDS OF MIXING

Taking an artist's idea in the form of raw audio tracks and mixing them to the best of your ability, making them shine, is an extremely rewarding skill to have. Even if you are mixing your own music, the joy it can bring to lift your song to a higher level through an awesome mix cannot be understated. However, if you are lucky enough to progress to a full-time position within the industry it's important to keep in mind the strain it places on your brainpower. Even if you are a keen hobbyist it's surprising how many hours you can rack up, so be careful too.

Mixing music can be mentally draining work. Please remember this and don't push yourself too hard. It will get easier the more knowledge you obtain and practice you put in. Try to learn to relax and think of the bigger picture rather than sweat the small things. Let the music bounce off you and react to emotional instincts rather than strain to hear every minute detail. Music should cause an automatic response in the subconscious depths of your soul. There should be some form of reaction in your body: a tapping foot, a bobbing

head or goosebumps perhaps. It shouldn't leave you with a headache and neck strain. If it does you are trying too hard. If you feel these symptoms, take a break and relax for ten minutes or so. Do everything you can to avoid the dreaded burnout that can affect musicians, songwriters and mix engineers alike.

I have a routine that I like to stick to weekdays and weekends. During the working week I see the three minutes and thirty seconds it takes to bounce down a mix as time to take an ear break. I return emails, phone calls or get something to drink. This doesn't sound like much but every little break or mind shift where you get out of your chair, stretch and think about something else adds up to a healthy day. I mentioned earlier that I switch the monitor gain up and down in volume all the time; this helps keep the ears fresher than you would if you pumped them all day with a maxed-out beat.

During the weekends I have a hobby to de-stress – I'm a woodworking weekend warrior! The saws I use are loud so I wear ear protection; whatever you do always protect your ears as they are your only connection to the magical, musical sound waves. Oh, and I don't listen to music!

So, keep happy, healthy and positive. A positive, can-do attitude will get you as far as anything else and before you know it you will have a 'Eureka!' moment when it all clicks into place and you take a huge leap forward.

I've had many such moments myself; it didn't happen overnight for me. My journey has been small steps with a few giant leaps. For example, in 2011 I learned about parallel compression. Wow, that was a giant leap for me and suddenly I had the drum sounds I'd been hearing and trying so hard to match. I don't know how you can get the smack of a snare drum without parallel compression. I take the parallel compression off and it sounds dull to me, like someone has put a towel over the drum. Also, meeting Chris Lord-Alge was a game-changer. He was checking out a mix of mine, and having him validate what I was doing reassured me that I was on the right path. I then grew in confidence, knowing that what I was doing wasn't 'wrong' and now, if it sounds good, I am confident enough to say it's right.

You too will have such events in your progression. Celebrate the good times when they happen, but also be aware of the negative thoughts too. We all have them; don't let them get you down but watch them float by as you focus on the task in hand and know that this is a lifelong journey of enlightenment with ever-moving goalposts. The moment you think you know it all is the moment you realize there is so much more to learn, and so it goes on. It's the nature of the beast, so look at it as a wonderful opportunity to soak up as much of this awesome craft as is possible.

I still listen to my heroes now and feel like I have a long way to go. I don't stress over it, I just do my thing and love every moment trying to do my best for the music in front of me.

MY MIXING HEROES

I recommend you study the work of other great mixers too – listen and learn. Ask yourself 'What makes them great? What are they doing that I should be doing too?' The answers are all there in your books of knowledge, i.e. the master wav or MP3 file, the CD, vinyl record or cassette tape. These are your references to learn by.

Here are my top five mixing heroes and why I admire them:

* Chris Lord-Alge: combines speed and efficiency.
* Kevin Churko: somehow manages to create space around his drums, the like of which I have never heard before.
* Randy Staub: master of the 'huge' mix.
* Mike Shipley: created some of the biggest larger-than-life drum sounds.
* Lynn Peterzell: the best mix engineer in country music in my opinion. When I moved to Nashville, I wanted to be him someday.

Here I am pictured with one of my heroes, Chris Lord-Alge. Meeting him, and having him tell me that what I was doing was correct, gave me a huge lift.

8
MASTERING

OVERVIEW

What is mastering? The answer to that question has changed throughout the years. At the inception of mainstream recording, there was no mastering to speak of, just one seamless process of capturing performances that were recorded direct to a wax disc. There were no separate recording, mixing and mastering stages. Then, as technology evolved, and the ways in which music could be recorded and delivered to the public became more advanced, a final stage of quality control and careful preparation of each release for the format it was to be delivered on became paramount.

This definition has remained true. Mastering can be thought of as taking a mix and preparing it for the intended delivery format. However, nowadays, mastering can be an integral extension of the mixing process, should the user choose it to be.

In years past, mix engineers haven't had the tools available to tackle the task of mastering, but all that has now changed. Anyone can now master their own mixes and it isn't as hard as you may think. All you need is a little knowledge, a positive attitude and the right mental approach.

It's true, a lot of the songs I mix get passed on to a professional mastering house, but then a lot of them don't. It's the client's decision at the end of the day. I still have to be able to provide a product that comes close to pro-mastering to those who either can't afford it or, for other reasons, such as tight deadlines, choose not to access it. All through my career I've been appreciative of the support of not only the big labels but also all the

singer-songwriters of Nashville and beyond who keep coming back again and again, mix after mix. I always say to them, 'You won't miss a pitch because of Billy Decker'. I will always meet a deadline no matter what and a big part of that is being able to master within my DAW.

There are still situations where a separate mastering stage will be required (if, for example, you are taking a collection of songs and presenting them as an EP or album) but for the purpose of this book we are talking about taking a single mix and bringing it up to current benchmark standards for our intended format – the 16-bit 44.1kHz wav file – all of which we can and will master within our DAW. So how do we do it?

When mastering my own mixes, it is always my intention to get as close to the results of a professional mastering engineer as I can. Make this your goal too. Don't settle for anything less. Always do the best you possibly can within your current levels of expertise. You will continually improve as you practise and refine your results and decisions.

I mentioned that the mixing and mastering processes can once again become entwined and mixing through your mastering chain with a positive mental approach will get you a long way. If you could hear my mixes with and without any of my pseudo mastering applied, the mastered version would be just a little wider, deeper and louder – that's it. It all starts with the mix. I set out to nail my mix every time in the best way I possibly can and that carries forward to the mastering stage. That is so important and I cannot reiterate it enough. A great mastered sound comes firstly from the mix and mastering should in no way change the balance of the mix. A bad mix can't be saved by mastering no matter how good the engineer is.

If I send a mix out to a pro-mastering house I expect it to come back a little wider, deeper and louder, just as I try to do at my studio. I tell them, 'Don't screw up my mix', and a good mastering house will be sympathetic to my request.

Think of our mastering within a DAW as this:

1. Nail the mix with your decisions making the mix as big, wide and deep as it can possibly be. This will transfer to a great master.
2. Don't break the mix with mastering. Instead, look to take it up a level. Mastering is the last chance you will have to affect your mix. Be sympathetic to the mix. Look to add extra loudness, depth and width while still being pleasing.

THE MASTERING CHAIN

Having already done so much within our template to manage levels and optimize the audio flowing through the channels, and assuming we've made

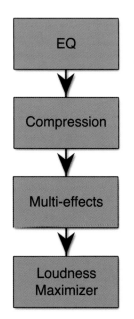

My mastering chain is always enabled and I mix through it without exception.

every effort to make our mix the best it can be, how can we polish our mix and move it one step closer to the modern requirements of the digital delivery format? The answer lies in the manipulation of the master-channel plugins and their gain staging. These plugins found on our master channel are our tools for mastering. Whatever plugin we place on the master channel will have a big impact on the overall sound of our mix, as the mix as a whole is affected.

Always treat the master channel carefully and don't insert any plugin that isn't absolutely necessary. So, let us take another look at our chain of master-channel plugins.

Firstly, an EQ tidies up the top and bottom end, then a buss compressor glues the mix together. A touch of magic dust is applied by a multi-effects plugin, then a final loudness maximizer brings the mix up to mastered levels to give us a representation of the final product, but we can deactivate this when exporting if the mastering of our mix is to be outsourced.

There are a few points I'd like to expand on and I feel it is definitely worth the time to recap what the plugins are and what they do within this mastering chapter. It is worth mentioning, to avoid any ambiguity, that I always mix through this mastering chain, so I always have this chain set up and enabled on my mastering channel. I recommend you do the same.

EQ

The first plugin in our template is an EQ module. All the EQ is doing is rolling off the low and top end. This is really important as it cleans up all the wasted energy on the top and bottom of the frequency spectrum, but in its default state this is all it is doing. However, you can think of mastering as the final chance you have to change any aspect of your mix. This EQ is the final chance to sweeten your master EQ curve, but be very careful when using it; use it wisely and gently as any changes here will affect all the instruments within any chosen band. Remember, it is vital that you never upset the balance of your mix with mastering, but it could be that you've made every attempt to make your mix as big and as wide as possible, and when referencing your chosen commercial master, there is a need to balance the overall EQ curve to bring your mix more in line. In this case, additional EQ is the answer. At this stage less is always more whatever the process and EQ is no different, so always switch the plugin in and out to check your decisions and always ask yourself, 'Is it really necessary at all?'

COMPRESSION

The second plugin is a buss compressor, which controls the dynamics of the overall mix. As with all the plugins on the master channel, any change here will affect the mix as a whole, so again be very careful with any changes you make and always check your changes by alternating between before and after states.

Some people claim they would never put a compressor on their master channel, some love to add compression, but only after they've mixed and would never mix through one. This is the beauty of there being so many options and so many differing sounds and ideas. Nothing is good or bad, just different. The clichéd phrase, 'If it sounds good, it is good', always applies. Personally, though, I don't know how I'd get my sound without the compression and the magic boxes of my mastering chain.

As you will have seen, my go-to default settings for my compressor are a 2:1 ratio, with the slowest attack and fastest decay time. This lets as much of the attack as is possible through before the compressor clamps it down. Depending on the genre you are mixing, you might want to alter this slightly. For example, when mixing rock music, a higher ratio of 3:1 or 4:1 is fun for a tighter sound. Also, some rock mixers I know go for a 10ms attack and use the auto-release function. Whatever the settings you use, it is important to note that your music should just be 'kissing' the compressor's gain-reduction needle, i.e. the needle should be ticking in and out with the loudest peaks without ever showing more than a 3db gain reduction.

MASTERING MULTI-EFFECTS

The third plugin in our mastering chain is the tricky one. It is a multi-effects plugin for mastering, all wrapped up in one convenient, easy-to-use box. See Appendix B if you want to know what brand I use, and if you own it already, great – you'll know all about it, but for the purpose of this exercise I will try to explain what's going on inside so that anyone who doesn't have it in their collection can get similar results by inserting additional processors.

So, what would I do if I had to master without my magic box? Well my chain of processors would be this:

1. A second buss compressor
2. A valve saturation plugin
3. A brick-wall limiter/maximizer

Let's look at these in more detail.

Second buss compressor

I would look to insert a second buss compressor (this is in addition to our previous compression plugin), but this time to be used as a parallel compressor, so look for one that has a mix dial on it, i.e. the ability to mix the compressed signal back in with the uncompressed signal in a parallel compression way (see page 39 for an explanation of parallel compression). Set the ratio, attack and release as per the first compressor and dial the mix function to 35 per cent. As this is parallel compression to be mixed back with the original signal we can hit it harder, set to your tastes.

Valve saturation plugin

Find a valve saturation plugin that simulates the way analogue devices such as tape recorders and valve circuits warm up your audio. If possible, use a plugin that again has a mix function and set the mix to 35 per cent.

Brick-wall limiter

Thirdly, insert a mastering-style, brick-wall maximizer/limiter and make sure the signal clips at some stage during playback. Set the output to 0.6db.

You can see we are blending the first two processors in with the original signal to minimize the effects of the processing, but adding enough in to bring additional punch and warmth that's missing without them, and then optimizing the audio through a limiter/maximizer. If you don't have plugins with a mix dial to give parallel compression you will need to set up the parallel compression in the traditional method.

Look to find the most transparent compressors and limiters you can find. The key here is to add additional punch, warmth and loudness to what we already have with minimal colouration.

LOUDNESS MAXIMIZER

The final mastering plugin is a loudness maximzer to bring overall control to the final level that is output when using the export function. Any plugin that is described as a loudness maximizer will do. Often, little user interaction is permitted or needed with these types of plugin. Normally, as a minimum, there is an input control, an output control and a method of converting the bit-length of your audio.

The more you overdrive the input the more limiting is taking place and the more your pristine master will be crushed and degraded, so be careful. I recommend setting the input threshold to -0.4db and the output to -0.1db and I like to see no more than 1db of gain reduction taking place at any stage. We are just taking that final step to bring the level up a touch, nothing major!

I deactivate this final plugin if I am sending the mix to be mastered elsewhere, but if I'm providing a mastered file to my client then this is where I'll dither down to 16 bits.

Remember to insert a dithering plugin in your final effects slot if your peak limiter/maximizer doesn't have the ability to dither to 16 bits, assuming you are exporting to a 16-bit 44.1kHz CD Industry Standard file and are not just concerned with HD playback.

THE LOUDNESS WAR

I am sure you already know all about the loudness war. It is one of the most talked about subjects in recent times within the music business. If you don't know then very briefly: back in the day, record labels realized that if they mastered their artists' songs louder than competitors they would be perceived as sounding better and therefore more desirable by the record-buying public. Initially, this paid off, but as playback levels were pushed way beyond realistic boundaries in the pursuit of *the* loudest mix, quality issues became more and more obvious.

We touched on this subject when looking at equalizing and balancing sounds. In audio production louder sounds better so each release became louder than the last until all the life had been crushed out of the music by compressing, limiting and clipping all the goodness out of the mix, producing masters that looked like solid bricks.

To fully illustrate this, both of the previous waveforms show the same mix. It is a pretty full-on mix with lots going on. The top waveform has been mastered to a conservative level for rock music. The bottom of the two waveforms has been mastered to the point of collapse and has a brick-like quality. The audio quality in the second, crushed master has been greatly diminished purely for the purpose of loudness, as has been the policy throughout the loudness war years.

Everyone agreed that this degrading of audio was benefiting no one, especially the end listener, so technology was developed to automatically compensate for louder mixes by turning them down whilst turning quiet mixes up. The use of this technology in playback systems such as audio-streaming websites is now so widespread that it negates the purpose of a loud mix; that and the

The classic brick waveform which is a common result of the loudness war.

decline of CD multi-disc players. So, the loudness war is, to all intents and purposes, now over. You don't have to make your mixes loud any more, but the fear of not sounding as loud as the rest is something that will stay with us, I'm sure.

Don't get me wrong, I love loudness. I mix loud and I master loud. I want my masters to be as loud as the next guy or gal's, but I also want the music to shine through, which is why I use a lot of small amounts of compression, limiting and signal maximization all over the mix rather than slamming it at the mastering stage. The result is a loud mix that is made louder by the mastering chain without destroying the mix. You'll see and hear this in your template. Your masters will be loud without compromise but true to your mix.

Metering Systems

How do you know when loud is too loud? The first warning signs should come from your ears and brain. Alarm bells will ring when you become sensitized to the effects of pushing too hard. To help you learn the properties of sound levels there are many plugins available that will visually assist you in assessing the loudness of both your mix and master. These are known as meters. Meters are used to measure the units of sound and have been around for as long as music or the spoken word has been captured. Meters can be used on any channel or between plugins on a single chain and can be an invaluable aid if you are just starting to familiarize yourself with the levels of sound. How do you know if a signal is too loud? A meter will tell you. As well as being able to place an individual meter at any point in your mix and master channels, every plugin will have its own inbuilt meter that will turn red if you push too much. This can be seen as a warning sign that all is not well, but as we'll see in the next chapter, red warning lights don't always need to be adhered to. My mixes have red lights all over them! The important issue is to know when to act and when to ignore.

I don't use any specific level meters to help judge the loudness of my mix, masters or individual channels. I've been doing this for so long now I just know,

but that doesn't mean you shouldn't use them. My advice would be to use meters until you are 100 per cent confident you can work without them. Which meter you use is up to you; do your research and familiarize yourself with the different types of meter and settle on your preference. Whatever type and brand you choose keep your metering consistent so your output is steady. Consistency is a sign of professionalism that will keep your clients or listeners coming back time and time again.

OTHER MASTERING TOOLS

We started this chapter by recognizing that mastering can now be thought of as a seamless part of mixing. Therefore, the tools we spoke of during the mixing chapter and the processes for assessing your mix apply to the mastering stage too. As you mix through the master-channel chain you will see that it is indeed one seamless process should you choose it to be. That doesn't mean that you can't separate the mixing and the mastering into separate sessions; if that works better for you then great, but with our template set up the way it is you don't have to.

Assuming you are mixing through your master plugins as I'd recommend, all the skills that we talked about regarding checking how a mix travels by listening on different speakers, EQ matching and spectrum analysis apply to the final master stage too. Build your own method of using all the tools available to you as you work your master towards the goal of matching the level of professionalism of commercial releases.

You will have learned from this chapter and the plugins on our master channel that all we are doing is adding a touch of compression, warmth and optimizing the loudness. We are not even changing the EQ curve unless it is absolutely necessary. All our decisions are taken within the mix. Get it right in the mix and your master should be just a louder, warmer, more glued-together version of the same thing.

9
OTHER CONSIDERATIONS

In this penultimate chapter I would like to address some other aspects of a mix, both inside and outside of your DAW and the digital world, that can influence your results. I'll move on to these shortly but first I'd like to put everything into perspective by reminding you not to sweat the small stuff.

DON'T SWEAT THE SMALL STUFF

Every tiny detail will seem important to you until you learn to relax in front of your monitors, to sit back and let the music hit your ears and tell you what it wants you to do. Let your instincts react accordingly. There are so many different points along the lifespan of a recorded performance that are subject to change that worrying about them all and trying to control them is just not feasible.

Let us think for a moment about the journey that just one track of our multi-track mixing project has taken to be with us today. We'll take a single acoustic guitar part as an example. From its conception the artist envisages how they would like it to sound. The producer, if there is one, will also have different ideas that they will put forward. They will then try a couple of different guitars and play the part in various areas of the neck whilst trying out alternative strumming and picking styles before settling on a final choice. Just these few decisions alone have a massive impact. Now to the choice of microphone – they may try two or three of their favourites before settling on one (or two for a stereo recording). Then they will look at

the mic position and decide on the right space and recording environment – see how the choices are stacking up? Every twist and turn takes the recording in a slightly different direction. Then there are the pre-amps and the outboard chain to consider, whether to add processors and effects whist tracking or leave them until later, all this before the part is commited to tape (or disc), and don't get me started on string gauge! This is all prior to our receiving the data within a multi-track format where we can start our decision-making and alterations.

You can see how many times during the recording and mixing of a musical performance that it is subject to change either by design or accident, and that is just one track! Multiply that by forty-eight for a 48-track recording and you start to get a perspective on the enormity of possibilities that exist and realize that we have to let go and not sweat the small stuff!

Look at the bigger picture. Realize that a vast multitude of decisions have already been made to get to the mixing stage we are now at. Don't feel you have to try to create a dramatic whirlwind of production gimmicks or reinvent the sounds already on offer. Simple decisions are called for. A clear head, confidence and an unfaltering determination to do what is right for the music. Improve without too much perceived change. Optimizing, clearing space and making pathways for sound will be enough to put smiles on faces. Mix with freedom and passion in broad brushstrokes, don't look back, have fun, enjoy the experience and most importantly, don't sweat the small stuff!

ROOMS: THE SPACE YOU MIX IN

The room that you mix in will have an impact on the outcome of your mix. Depending on who you speak to, your room could be *the* biggest factor in the quality of your mix. The good news is that every space can be improved with a little effort, and adapting to your room whilst you mix is a natural development you will go through. You will naturally change what you do inside your studio as you hear how your mixes travel outside of your studio.

It's important to remember that no two spaces are identical, and not one of them has ever been perfect. Yet glorious mixes exist regardless of this fact. Every mix that has ever graced a vinyl disc, cassette tape or CD, whether the song has gone on to sell a million copies or been left gathering dust on a forgotten mixtape, has been mixed within its own unique, imperfect environment, and you too can create a glorious mix whatever the shape and size of your room.

Acceptance is the key here. There is no such thing as the perfect room. Never has been, never will be. It simply cannot happen. Yes, the more money you throw at a room the closer to perfect your imposed house EQ curve will be (assuming you make the right decisions), but there will still remain imperfections within the room when analyzed, and every time you move your head to a different listening position the response of the room will change.

Even if you could create the perfect room, the very fact that objects such as mixing desks stand between the monitors and your ears means that those pristine sound waves will have been coloured by the time they reach your ears. Colouration occurs when secondary waves bounce off the nearby walls and objects and reach your ears at a slightly later time than the direct sound. The delay is not long enough for the brain to perceive the many reflections as separate sounds – instead it combines the direct sound and early reflections into one complete wave. A side-effect of this phenomenon is the colouration we know as phase cancellation or reinforcement.

Every room from the very best million-dollar studios around the world to the small bedrooms of the new breed of talent is imperfect, so don't stress yourself chasing perfection. There is no such thing. Everything is a compromise.

We have established that we can't have perfection so what can we do to make sure our mixes become the best they can possibly be with regards to the environment around us? We can analyze, add acoustic treatment, listen and adapt.

The subject of studio design and acoustic treatment is a vast and complicated topic that can easily fill a book on its own, but there are, however, some rules that are generally accepted and acknowledged to improve critical listening conditions. I will, therefore, provide you with a nudge in the right direction and tell you what I do.

If you are constructing your mix room from the foundations up, I will assume you are hiring the services of a pro or have carried out extensive research to collate all the resources and tools you require. Building a studio can require a serious investment of time and money and is easy to get wrong if you don't approach it in a professional manner.

If you haven't the time, energy or inclination to build your own studio, simply follow these tried-and-tested guidelines and make the best of what you have.

If you are lucky enough to have a few different rooms to choose from then the first task is to measure all three dimensions (length, width and height). Shoot for the biggest room but also the room that has the most uneven proportions between length, width and height whist still being symmetrical. This will give the fewest problems. A small, square room is as bad as it gets, as certain sound waves double up to reinforce whilst others cancel each other out. This will happen in every room to a certain extent but is lessened in rooms of unrelated dimensions. If you only have one room available it is still important to measure the exact dimensions as we will need those in a moment.

Another important consideration is the sound coming in and leaking out of your mix room. If you are recording as well as mixing then you don't want car horns and overhead planes making cameo appearances. But equally important may be controlling noise leaving your room if, for example, you work unsociable hours and have attached neighbours or resident family members that need sleep. So choose well.

Once you have decided on your room, remove everything that is possible to remove, including anything that will rattle or vibrate. Then, with an empty room you can turn your thoughts to the position of the workstation, monitors and acoustic treatment.

Firstly, where to place yourself and your monitors? There are a few rules that I recommend you adhere to. Symmetry is the key here; the monitors and your central seating position should each mark the three points of an equilateral triangle. Therefore, place your monitors equidistant to a central point along the shortest wall (read the monitor manual for the optimum placement regarding distance from the wall), moving them and your seating position as far apart as possible, whilst still retaining the three points of your triangle. Then set the height of the monitors so that the tweeters are aimed at a point immediately behind your ears – it may help to envisage the tweeters firing a laser beam through your ears. Then finally move your workstation into a comfortable central working position. This set-up will give the best stereo image possible. If, for any reason, you cannot achieve the equilateral triangle method, then moving yourself forwards or backwards, whilst keeping a central position to the monitors, will provide the best alternative monitoring solution.

With the monitors and workstation in place it's time to think about acoustic treatment. It is probably fair to say that the more time and money you spend on treating your room the better the results will be. However, there can be a point where you overdo it and kill the room. My best advice would be to buy a ready-made complete treatment system, if your budget will allow it, or make

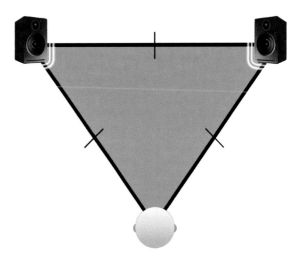

Equilateral Triangle

Position yourself and your monitors on the three points of an equilateral triangle.

your own and add a little at a time until your room sounds great to you. If you are making your own traps try a combination of absorption and diffusion and focus on all known problem areas first, these being the area behind the monitors, the corners of the room and all the first reflection points. The usual way to find a first reflection point is by asking a friend to hold a mirror close to the side walls. Any point from which you can see the monitors in the mirror when seated in your listening position is a first reflection point. These are located on ceilings and floors also, so be sure to trap these too.

My current workspace is a mix room at the Westwood Studio, Nashville. I've always rented a mix room as I love to get out and about and feel like I'm part of the music-making community. For me it's an important part of networking, being seen and letting people know I'm here. It's a great way to meet and keep clients.

For seventeen years, I worked from a mix room at a studio called Sound Stage, until I recently moved to my very minimalist studio at Westwood.

The look of my room is like a log cabin. There's something about wood and audio that sounds good together. I did most of the acoustic treatment myself. I built a sound-absorption cloud above the desk and some of the baffles, all using my woodworking skills. I then trapped the corners, placed the monitors as far apart as I could whilst staying within the three points of the equilateral triangle rule, and just made it look cool. It ended up sounding pretty awesome.

All I have in my room is an old Avid Pro Control mixing desk, monitors and a boombox. I'm 100 percent in-the-box and don't use the Avid Pro Control, other than as a volume button for the monitors. But having it in the room makes me feel like I'm sitting at a console and also helps to impress clients as well as looking good in photos. For the very occasional overdub I have a recording booth, with an SSL X-Logic channel strip, and an Audio Technica AT4033 microphone – that's it!

COMPUTER SPECIFICATION, OPERATING SYSTEMS AND UPGRADING

At the time of writing I am using Pro Tools 10, but this is not the most up-to-date version. The latest version is Pro Tools 12 but I refuse to upgrade until it is absolutely necessary. My current version is stable and I have everything I need to mix every quality moment of each day. All my friends who have Pro Tools 12 (and 11) are always complaining about crashes and incompatibility problems so I'll stick with version 10 until I'm forced to upgrade.

It's the man or woman and not the machine that counts; you'll make great music on whatever system you have. Spending frustrated hours thinking of what you haven't got or wasting precious mixing time with upgrades you do not need will only be detrimental to your output. Put the hours in practising all that we have talked about in this book and you will soon see improvements.

However, having said that the machine doesn't count, I feel it only right that I include my machine spec for completeness so here it is:

- Computer: Apple Mac
- Operating System: OS X version 10.9.2
- Processor: 2.66 GHz Quad-Core Intel Xeon
- Memory: 10 GB 1066 MHz DDR3

SAMPLE RATES

Unlike the continuous analogue sound waves that reside outside of your DAW and bounce around us every moment as we live and breathe, your computer processes music by taking a single snapshot of the analogue waveform many times per second, and playing those snapshots back in sequence to create an illusion of continuity. This is exactly the same as the movies you watch on TV; the picture seems to be one unbroken stream but is in fact made up of many still photographs that are projected in sequence at a speed too fast for the eye to notice it is being fooled.

The sample rate with regards to audio can, therefore, be defined as the number of times a single sample (a musical still photograph) of an audio stream is recorded per second. It is measured in Hz or kHz. The most common sampling rate that people are aware of is the replay rate of a CD – 44,100 samples per second (44,100Hz or 44.1kHz).

For mixing purposes what I do, and what I suggest you do, is always keep the mix in the sampling rate you are given. I never ever change the sampling rate of a project. I let the mastering engineer take it down to 44.1kHz for CDs or my DAW will convert it when I bounce down to stereo if I'm producing the master, which it's worth pointing out is always in-the-box but in real time.

If you are mixing for clients, go with the sampling rate they chose. If you are mixing your own music do your research and stick to one sampling rate for all your projects but, honestly, don't stress over it, none of your end listeners will be any the wiser, no one will listen and say, 'Oh man, if only they had used 48kHz instead of 44.1kHz!' Whatever you settle on will be fine.

BIT DEPTH

While the sampling rate we talked about before is the frequency of sampling, i.e. how many times a single sample is taken per second, the bit depth of audio can be thought of as the size of one individual digital sample, i.e. the number of bits of information each sample holds (one sample being a single snapshot of our analogue waveform as it is converted from analogue to digital information by our analogue-to-digital converters in a computer's soundcard).

This is important to know as it correlates directly to the degree of dynamic range available to us and the amount of headroom we have in our mix. Put simply, the higher the bit rate the more headroom, which is important as it gives us the space we need to combine our multi-track recordings without hitting the dreaded digital ceiling – the ceiling in the digital domain being 0dBFS. I'll offer a quick explanation of this as it relates to how I work and suggest you follow the same principles, but again look to your manual for more detail.

DBFS is the digital scale that represents the level of sound in decibels relative to full scale. Full scale is the term we give to the digital ceiling beyond which it is impossible to go any further. So, signals that are louder than 0dBFS will get played back but (and this where the bit depth comes into play) only the part of the wavelength that falls within the allowance of the bit depth of the sample will be heard.

To clarify this: a 16-bit sample has the capacity to hold a maximum number of bits. It can only ever calculate up to this maximum number, and if our sample exceeds the maximum allowable it will not reproduce the correct waveform. Clip-

ping of the waveform will occur at the point that its limitations are reached. This is what we know as digital distortion. To anyone who has pushed 16-bit recording gear into the red this sound will be familiar as a horrible noise to be avoided at all costs. But the good news is that increasing the bit size (thus increasing the capacity of information our sample can hold) pushes up the digital ceiling to the point where it becomes impossible for us to breach it. It, in effect, becomes irrelevant at 24 bits and higher.

And why is this important? Did I mention I mix hot? I mix very hot and should you choose to follow everything I've laid out in this book, you will too. When I mix there are red lights going off here, there and everywhere. It doesn't matter within the realms of our mix as we are protected by 24 bits or more. However, you may want to check the individual plugins. Each plugin has its own inbuilt meter that shows a red light when overdriven. Whether that equates to digital distortion or not depends on the design of the plugin in question. Let your ears be the decision-makers. If it sounds good, it is good. Can you hear any distortion? If not then don't worry. I have red lights all over my plugins but it doesn't bother me if I can't hear anything going on. In fact, some plugins are designed to be pushed into the red in true analogue style. Your friend, the plugin manual, holds the answers. Get to know it well.

Having said red lights don't matter, there is one exception to this rule, and that is the master channel. You never want to see red lights on the master channel. It won't have an impact whilst mixing at 24 bits or more because adequate headroom is available. You won't think anything is wrong, but the problem will rear its ugly head when you bounce down to 16 bits. If you do have red warning lights on the master channel then the parts of the audio causing the red lights to flash will not be replicated faithfully when exporting and will instead be clipped, and will be heard as digital distortion.

Here is a quick fun exercise you can do to prove this and become aware of its implications.

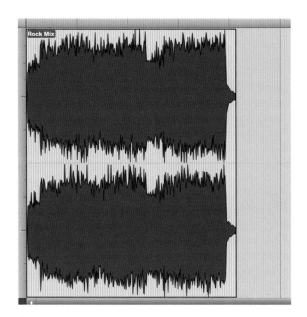

Step 1: Import a full mix that peaks at 0 dbfs at one point during the song. It is okay to normalize a mix for this exercise as quality is not an issue.

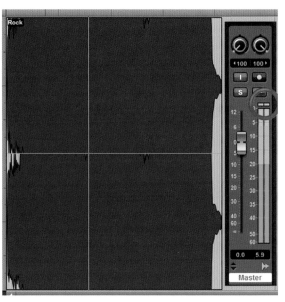

Step 2: Apply a +6 db boost to the waveform using the clip gain tool or similar. The waveform of the song will now be clipping the master buss.

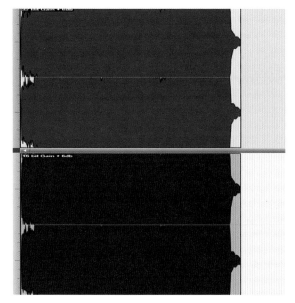

Step 3: Export the song in (a) 24 or 32 bit and (b) 16 bit. Import these files back into a clean session and they will both look like identical clipped house bricks!

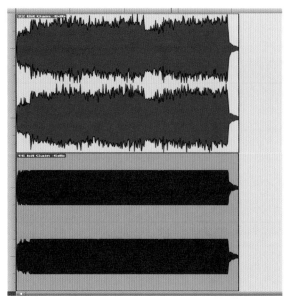

Step 4: Reduce both sound files back to their original level by applying a -6 db cut and you will see that only the 16 bit export has in fact been clipped.

To summarize: the 24-bit export looked like it was clipped, yet there was no distortion on playback. Lowering the clip gain of the sound file revealed that all its wonderful peaks were completely intact.

When we did the same for the 16-bit file it looked clipped, it sounded distorted, and it was most definitely clipped. Bringing the clip gain down to reveal the full waveform showed that the mix retained the appearance of a house brick and sounded horrible. Why? Because 16 bits are not enough to hold all the information required to faithfully recreate high levels of sound, but 24 bits or more are.

IN CLOSING

You now have all the tools to go forth and mix a no. 1 record in-the-box just as I did. However, I cannot give you a no. 1 song to mix. That is up to you. Go forth and find the magic that separates the hits from the misses. Lots of luck is also involved, but you now have the knowledge to present a top-class professional mix when that luck does strike.

Thank you for reading this book and entrusting me with your time to learn. I hope you have found it helpful. Never give up learning and progressing on your own personal journey, and one day you will look back and realize you are a pro mixer up with the best. You won't know when it happened and you won't be aware of it in the moment, but one day you will look back and smile. You will have made it. All the lost days, the dead-end roads, the self-doubt will suddenly have been worth it.

So, go and practise, practise and practise some more. Learn to use this new template blindfolded and become part of the machine. Amaze onlookers as you fly around your mouse and keyboard like a magician with his trusty wand. Discover new ways, new talents and make your future a past you can look back on without any regrets. Always give 100 per cent without trying too hard. Imagine it means nothing when it means everything. Relax, breathe, and let the music talk to you as it hits your senses and rocks your instincts. Most importantly, always keep the balance between work and family; and last but not least, just have fun!

ABOUT BILLY DECKER

I am including a few lines about myself and my career, not to brag about my past successes but to say, 'Hey, this is who I am and this is what I've done'. In doing this you can be assured that I know my way around a mix through many years of honest hard work and discovery. I've had my own personal journey, my ups and downs, my problems to overcome and my answers to find in exactly the same way as you are doing now. I've made my mistakes, too, so you don't have to.

I was born Billy Decker and raised in Nebraska, USA, on 28 August 1967. I studied at the University of Nebraska and graduated with a Bachelor of Science degree in Criminal Justice. However,

I saw my future within the music industry. I really believed I could succeed if I studied my craft, so I enrolled at the Full Sail University for Recording Arts in 1992 and went on to be graduation salutatorian.

In 1994 I moved to Nashville and began my working life as a staff writer, penning songs for a music publisher before deciding to focus 100 per cent on mixing. I was already mixing demos for songwriters so I put the word out that in the future I was only going to mix, and I've been mixing in Nashville ever since!

I am proud to say I have mixed multiple Billboard no. 1 singles and sold over twenty-five million albums. I'm the guy in Nashville that record

Here I am pictured with recording artist Rodney Atkins and producer Ted Hewitt.

A fun banner we had made after Rodney Atkins' fourth straight number one single, 'Cleaning This Gun.'

labels trust to get them 'that radio-friendly sound'. I've mixed songs for artists such as Chris Young, Dustin Lynch, Rodney Atkins, Kenny Chesney, Darius Rucker, Billy Ray Cyrus, George Jones, Jamie Lynne Spears and Sam Hunt – to name a few.

The mixes I'm best known for are within country music but I mix all types of music. For example, I'm a big fan of metal music, which I love to mix too. I mix around 1,000 songs across all genres each year. Many of these songs don't hit the no. 1 spot but are still great mixes and they all have one thing in common – my mix template. A mix template that you too can use for whatever music bangs your drum. Remember, a good balance is a good balance no matter what the musical style.

I really wanted to share the experience and knowledge I've accumulated and have enjoyed giving you the tools to be able to mix to a professional standard fast. Practise the methods you've learned in this book and in no time at all you'll see big improvements in the quality of your output. As I have said before, we are not trying to put men or women on the moon; we are just trying to put them on the radio.

I believe life is all about balance. If something is out of balance, everything else is out of whack. Get your home life in order and all of a sudden your phone starts ringing, the money starts rolling in and everything falls into place. So, have some fun but don't spend so long on your mixes that you miss out on the finer things in life. My mixes generally take me around forty-five minutes and now you've set up your template you should aim to mix your songs in around an hour too. Use the rest of the time to let your clients tweak their mix. Get them involved. After all, you get to move onto another project, but they have to live with this for the rest of their lives! Help them to make the best record you possibly can and, trust me, they will always come back and, most importantly, tell their friends and spread the word.

And in case you're wondering how I got the name 'the Deckerator', well this came about when a songwriter asked me to 'deckerate' his music as a joke and it has kind of stuck with me ever since.

Should you wish to reference my mixes you can find my complete discography on www.allmusic.com – search for Billy Decker or Bill Decker. You can find a link pointing the way on my website, www.billydecker.com.

APPENDIX A

MIXING DESK CHANNELS

Channel	Name		
		22	SNR Par
		23	Bass
1	J-KIK	24	AG L
2	D-KIK	25	AG R
3	H-KIK	26	EG 1 L
4	Cym Rev	27	EG 1 R
5	SNR Top	28	EG 2 L
6	SNR Bot	29	EG 2 R
7	Fatty	30	Steel
8	Mid	31	B3
9	High	32	Piano
10	Verb	33	Synth 1
11	HT06	34	Synth 2
12	Tom 1	35	I Delay
13	Tom 2	36	I Verb
14	Tom 3	37	Phas
15	OH L	38	Vox 1
16	OH R	39	Vox 2
17	Room	40	BV 1
18	Tamb	41	BV 2
19	DS Dry	42	BV Sub
20	DS PC	43	V Verb
21	DS 11	44	V Delay

APPENDIX B

PLUGIN EFFECTS AND PROCESSORS

Plugin	Name	Manufacturer	Type
1.	Trigger	Slate Digital	Drum replacement
2.	SSL E-Channel	Waves	SSL console emulation
3.	Trigger	Slate Digital	Drum replacement
4.	Trigger	Slate Digital	Drum replacement
5.	Channel Strip 3	Metric Halo	Channel strip emulation
6.	SSL E-Channel	Waves	SSL console emulation
7.	JST Clip	Joey Sturgis Tones	Peak clipper
8.	Channel Strip 3	Metric Halo	Channel strip emulation
9.	Trigger	Slate Digital	Drum replacement
10.	SSL E-Channel	Waves	SSL console emulation
11.	Trigger	Slate Digital	Drum replacement
12.	Channel G	McDSP	Console emulation
13.	Trigger	Slate Digital	Drum replacement
14.	SPL Transient Designer	Universal Audio	Transient controller
15.	Trigger	Slate Digital	Drum replacement
16.	L3 Ultramaximizer	Waves	Peak limiter/maximizer
17.	Channel Strip 3	Metric Halo	Channel strip emulation
18.	Trigger	Slate Digital	Drum replacement
19.	Filterbank P4	McDSP	Equalizer
20.	Trigger	Slate Digital	Drum replacement
21.	Filterbank P4	McDSP	Equalizer
22.	Trigger	Slate Digital	Drum replacement
23.	Filterbank P4	McDSP	Equalizer
24.	SSL E-Channel	Waves	SSL console emulation
25.	SSL E-Channel	Waves	SSL console emulation
26.	Trueverb	Waves	Reverb
27.	L2 Ultramaximizer	Waves	Peak limiter/maximizer
28.	Impact	Avid	Compressor
29.	Compressor Bank3	McDSP	Compressor
30.	Analog Channel	McDSP	Analogue circuitry emulation
31.	Retro Limiter	McDSP	Vintage limiter
32.	JST Clip	Joey Sturgis Tones	Peak clipper

Plugin	Name	Manufacturer	Type
33.	Oxford EQ	Sonnox	Equalizer
34.	JST Clip	Joey Sturgis Tones	Peak clipper
35.	1975 Compressor	URS	Compressor
36.	FabFilter	Pro-Q	Equalizer
37.	Oxford EQ	Sonnox	Equalizer
38.	MaxxBass	Waves	Bass enhancement technology
39.	Channel Strip 3	Metric Halo	Channel strip emulation
40.	CLA-76	Waves	Compressor/limiter
41.	L2 Ultramaximizer	Waves	Peak limiter/maximizer
42.	Channel Strip 3	Metric Halo	Channel strip emulation
43.	CLA-76	Waves	Compressor/limiter
44.	L2 Ultramaximizer	Waves	Peak limiter/maximizer
45.	BLT EQ	URS	Equalizer
46.	JST Clip	Joey Sturgis Tones	Peak clipper
47.	L2 Ultramaximizer	Waves	Peak limiter/maximizer
48.	BLT EQ	URS	Equalizer
49.	JST Clip	Joey Sturgis Tones	Peak clipper
50.	L2 Ultramaximizer	Waves	Peak limiter/maximizer
51.	BLT EQ	URS	Equalizer
52.	L2 Ultramaximizer	Waves	Peak limiter/maximizer
53.	BLT EQ	URS	Equalizer
54.	L2 Ultramaximizer	Waves	Peak limiter/maximizer
55.	Channel Strip 3	Metric Halo	Channel strip emulation
56.	L2 Ultramaximizer	Waves	Peak limiter/maximizer
57.	Channel Strip 3	Metric Halo	Channel strip emulation
58.	L2 Ultramaximizer	Waves	Peak limiter/maximizer
59.	Channel Strip 3	Metric Halo	Channel strip emulation
60.	L2 Ultramaximizer	Waves	Peak limiter/maximizer
61.	Channel Strip 3	Metric Halo	Channel strip emulation
62.	L2 Ultramaximizer	Waves	Peak limiter/maximizer
63.	Channel Strip 3	Metric Halo	Channel strip emulation
64.	L2 Ultramaximizer	Waves	Peak limiter/maximizer
65.	Echo Farm	Line 6	Delay and echo effects
66.	Renaissance Reverb	Waves	Reverb
67.	Doubler	Waves	Double-tracking effect
68.	CLA-76	Waves	Compressor/limiter
69.	Channel Strip 3	Metric Halo	Channel strip emulation
70.	Renaissance Vox	Waves	Vocal effects/maximizer
71.	DeEsser	Waves	De-esser
72.	DeEsser	Waves	De-esser
73.	CLA-76	Waves	Compressor/limiter
74.	Channel Strip 3	Metric Halo	Channel strip emulation
75.	Renaissance Vox	Waves	Vocal effects/maximizer
76.	DeEsser	Waves	De-esser

Plugin	Name	Manufacturer	Type
77.	DeEsser	Waves	De-esser
78.	CLA-76	Waves	Compressor/limiter
79.	Channel Strip 3	Metric Halo	Channel strip emulation
80.	Renaissance Vox	Waves	Vocal effects/maximizer
81.	DeEsser	Waves	De-esser
82.	DeEsser	Waves	De-esser
83.	Renaissance De-Esser	Waves	De-esser
84.	Renaissance Reverb	Waves	Reverb
85.	Echo Farm	Line 6	Delay and echo effects
86.	Oxford EQ	Sonnox	Equalizer
87.	Krammer PIE Compressor	Waves	Buss compressor
88.	Oxford Inflator	Sonnox	Loudness maximizer
89.	L3 Ultramaximizer	Waves	Peak limiter/maximizer

GLOSSARY

Absorption When music is played within a room, sound waves bounce around, reflecting off all surfaces. Not all of the sound is reflected, however. Some becomes absorbed into the materials found within the room. Absorption is the term used to describe this loss of sound energy and is found within reverberation effects and room measurement tools to specify the amount of sound that becomes absorbed.

Acoustics The scientific study of sound. Also a term used to describe the natural quality of a musical room. A 'live' room used for recording can be said to have good acoustics.

Analogue-to-digital converter A digital device that takes sound from the analogue world and digitizes the audio so that computing devices may process the music before returning it to the analogue world. A digital-to-analogue converter converts digital sound back to analogue.

ADSR envelope Describes the complete cycle of any one sound from its initial burst of energy back to silence. ADSR stands for Attack, Decay, Sustain and Release and describes how sound changes over time. The whole movement from initial transient to silence is often described as an envelope. The phrase is most common in synthesizer and keyboard sound design.

Air Describes the uppermost highs of the audio spectrum. Increasing the level of this range of frequencies can be said to give a sound more air.

Amplifier A device that increases the power of an audio signal and is often referred to simply as an amp. Amplifiers can be found in many forms within a recording studio from the device that amplifies an electric guitar to the amplifier that links the mixing desk to the monitor speakers. Devices such as monitors that have amplifiers built in are referred to as powered or active.

Amplitude The size of a vibration that results in a sound wave. The bigger the vibration, the deeper the wave and the louder the sound.

Analogue In sound engineering terms, analogue relates to the audio signal that exists as one unbroken physical sound wave and the equipment used to process this wave of frequencies.

Attack The very first initial burst of sound energy.

Attenuation The reduction of levels of sound.

Audio Can be used to describe any sound in general, but is more often used where sound is recorded and broadcasted.

Auxiliary send and return Often referred to simply as aux inputs and outputs; auxiliary connections are generally configured as additional sends and returns on an audio device (analogue or digital). The most common uses are to divert sound out of, and back into, a mixing desk via an effects unit in an effects loop or to feed the headphones of a recording artist (send only).

Balance Can have different meanings relating to mix engineering. Firstly, a balance dial can be found on a mixing desk to simultaneously control the levels of both the left and right channels in a stereo signal. Balance can also be used to describe the overall composition of a mix, i.e. the balance between all sounds. If a mix sounds wrong it is referred to as 'out of balance' whereas a good mix is a 'balanced mix'.

Band When relating to equalization, a band is the range of frequencies that one particular control affects. Equalizers may have many bands as with a graphic equalizer, or as few as two or three. A band may also be used to describe a group of musicians.

Bass   The lowest region of the frequency spectrum. Bass can be represented by frequency numbers, e.g., 64Hz, or spoken of in subjective terms such as 'punchy' or 'thumping'. Bass also relates to the instruments that form the foundation of music, such as a bass guitar or bass drum.

Bass enhancer   A bass enhancer is one particular type of effect that creates artificial bass frequencies to enhance existing ones. It uses psychoacoustic technology to fool the brain into thinking that bass frequencies are present when they are not. This is useful when playing music through small speakers.

Bell shape   A type of equalization curve, an equalization curve being the visual shape that is formed when a range of frequencies are either boosted or cut. A bell-shaped EQ is also referred to as a peaking EQ or parametric EQ.

Bit   The smallest unit of information used in computing, a bit is derived from the words 'binary digit'.

Bit depth   When relating to digital audio, bit depth means the number of bits of information that each sample contains (a sample being a digital snapshot of analogue sound at any given moment in time). CDs are able to accommodate 16 bits per sample, for example.

Boost   Used to denote an increase in the level of a signal or range of frequencies.

Brick-wall limiter   A type of limiter that restricts an audio signal to an absolute maximum level. The maximum level will never be breached and is controlled by the threshold setting. Most commonly placed on the master buss to safeguard against digital distortion.

Buss   Or 'bus' as the term is often written. A mixer channel or circuit that accepts more than one source. It can be thought of as a vehicle for audio, transporting multiple sounds together from one destination to another in one direction.

Buss compressor   A type of compressor that has been designed to work with a mixture of sounds blended together as one. As the name

suggests, a buss compressor works best when placed on a buss.

Cents   A measurement system for dividing the smallest musical interval, a semitone, into further subdivisions. There are 100 cents to a semitone and although it is impossible to hear the transition from one cent to another, cents still have an important role to play in sound design.

Channel   The path an audio signal takes when travelling from one location to another, commonly on a mixing desk and within a digital audio workstation. A channel carries one source in one direction. Mono is a one-channel format. Stereo is a two-channel format, carrying a left and a right signal.

Channel strip   A collective term to describe the various components that sit along a mixing desk's channel. From top to bottom, a channel strip may include an input level control, an equalizer, dynamics processors, a fader and output options. A channel strip is duplicated many times on a mixing desk, giving the impression that it is a complex beast, but closer inspection will show that much of the desk is one channel strip replicated again and again.

Chorus   Can be a musical section within a song ('Don't bore us, get to the chorus!' is a well-known phrase in songwriting). Alternatively, a chorus can be a type of effect, one that takes a signal, duplicates it and then intentionally alters the duplicate sound so that it is fractionally out of time and out of tune, before mixing it back in with the original sound. When performed correctly the effect thickens sounds in a pleasing manner.

Clip   When used within the context of a digital audio workstation, a clip is the part of recorded audio that is actually played back. Not all the sound that is recorded has to be heard. By specifying that only one section is replayed you are creating a clip. Alternatively, to clip audio is to push sound through the limits of the carrying device, which results in distortion.

Clipper   A type of sound processor that intentionally clips a sound source in a controlled manner to reduce the dynamic range of a signal. A clipper works much the same as a compressor or limiter but with subjectively fewer side effects.

Compression   Can be the act of reducing the dynamic range of a sound source, dynamic range being the difference between the quietest and loudest parts. Compression reduces the loudest peaks of a sound. The whole signal can then be boosted back up to pre-compression levels. The result is a more controlled, stable signal. Alternatively, compression can be used when discussing the reduction of the quantity of data when changing audio to a compressed format. MP3, for example, is a data-compression format.

Compressor   An audio processor that reduces the dynamic range of a sound source (see also Compression).

Console   Another word used to describe a mixing desk. Within a digital audio workstation context the term console emulation is often used to describe a plugin that claims to recreate the qualities of a physical mixing desk.

Crossover frequency   The dividing point at which the frequency spectrum is split, for whatever purpose. All speakers with more than one cone have a crossover frequency and equalizers contain crossover frequencies as different bands interact.

Cut   Another word for attenuation or reduction, or alternatively used to mean delete or mute.

DAW   An abbreviation of digital audio workstation, the all-in-one studio in a computer that musicians and engineers use to create musical compositions. Generally, but not always, a digital audio workstation will have two main windows; a tracking/editing window that replicates a multi-track recorder and a mixer window that recreates a physical mixing desk.

DBFS   An abbreviation of the term 'decibels relative to full scale'; a decibel is a unit of measurement for the level of sound, 'full scale' being the maximum peak level of a digital audio system.

Decay   The part of a sound that reduces after the initial attack; decay is a parameter commonly found in synthesizer sound design and effect plugins.

Decibel   A unit of measurement used to document the power of sound.

De-esser   An audio processor designed to reduce the sibilant consonants in a vocal performance. Although designed with vocals in mind, a de-esser can be used to reduce any problematic frequency that is within the range of the plugin.

Delay   To delay a signal or recorded track is to move it backwards in time. This could be for the purpose of aligning one sound recording to additional takes, or perhaps to create a time-based effect. A delay effect is a plugin that automatically records a signal and then plays it back at a later point in time. The delayed signal may be one echo or many repeated echoes.

Detune   A process that moves the pitch of a sound downwards. The amount of detuning applied can range from a few cents to many musical pitches or octaves.

Diffusion   To affect sound in a way that spreads the sound energy evenly across any given environment, be it real or virtual. Diffusion is a term used in room-analysis tools and reverberation plugins, for example.

Digital   Digital audio can be defined as sound that has passed through an analogue-to-digital converter or has been created synthetically by a digital sound engine. Basically, digital means digits have been used in the process – e.g., a computer uses the digits 1 and 0.

Digital Audio Workstation   *See* DAW.

Distortion   This happens as a result of pushing the level of sound beyond the limits of its replay system. Music can be distorted intentionally or by mistake. There are many distortion effects that change the sound of instruments such as guitars, but accidental digital distortion is generally to be avoided.

Dithering   The act of reducing the number of bits within a digital recording. The compact disc format only allows a maximum of 16 bits. Most music is created in 24- or 32-bit resolution. This means that during mastering a process must happen to allow for 16-bit CD playback (assuming a 16-bit format is the requirement). Dithering is that process.

Double-tracking A production technique whereby one musical part is performed and recorded twice in a near-identical fashion. The performance of both recordings must be as accurate as possible as any differences will cause distractions to the listening ear. When executed properly, double-tracking has a thickening effect on the audio.

Doubler Also known as a harmonizer. A type of plugin that simulates the double-track production technique (*see also* Double-tracking). One or more additional layers of doubling are automatically added without the need to perform and record each separate take.

Drive A form of distortion associated with analogue emulation plugins. The effect ranges from subtle to extreme. Also a control found on guitar pedals and amplifiers to overdrive the signal.

Drum replacer A plugin that automatically replaces one sound with another. Designed for use with drum performances, a drum replacer can actually play any sample loaded into its interface as a replacement for the incoming audio. There is generally an option to blend both source audio and triggered samples together.

Dry Describes a signal that is unprocessed by any effect or processor.

Dynamic range Describes the difference between the loudest and the quietest part of a sound recording.

Dynamics Relates to the difference in volume of a sound or note when compared to other sounds or notes.

Dynamics processors Processing modules that affect the dynamic range.

Early reflections Sound bursts forth from studio monitors at all angles and bounces off whatever lies in its path on its journey to the eardrum. The earliest bouncing waves that arrive in approximately the first thirty milliseconds (this varies per listener) are called early reflections and are perceived by the listener as being part of the original sound, not a separate echo.

Ears The most important piece of equipment in any audio chain or, to be more accurate, the brain and ears working together as one. Hear sound incorrectly and you will make the wrong decisions, you will hear problems that are not there and miss problems that are. Training your ears should be your priority.

Echo A time-delayed copy of an original sound that is repeated one or more times. The terms echo and delay can both be used to describe a time-delayed signal. Back in the day, the word echo was also associated with reverberation in an era when echo chambers existed in recording studios to generate natural reverberation.

Effect Any plugin that alters the state of a sound. More precisely, an effect adds a second altered wet copy of an original sound back to the original in a blend of the two. If the whole of the sound is changed by the plugin then this should be considered a processor.

Effects chain It is possible to send the output of one effect to the input of another. When this is done one or more times, the result is a chain of effects all linked on the same signal path, commonly known as an effects chain.

Emulation The act of trying to copy or imitate. Many plugins are designed as emulations of physical hardware. They can never be the exact article, but that does not mean they should be avoided, they are just different. Use your ears and follow your instinct to find the ones that best suit your style.

Equalizer An audio processor that alters the levels of specific frequencies within a sound or mix of sounds and can be thought of as a more detailed variation of the basic tone controls found on hi-fi systems. The word 'equalizer' is often abbreviated to 'EQ'.

Equilateral triangle A triangle in which all three sides are of equal length. Often used to form the best monitoring solution whereby the two monitors and the listener are placed on each of the three points of the imaginary triangle.

Expander Increases dynamic range, making quiet sounds quieter and louder sounds louder; the opposite of compression.

Export   To save audio as a new file under a new name. This could be a mixdown of a multi-track recording or individual tracks that are exported to be shared or used in other projects, for example.

Fade   This can be either a 'fade in' or 'fade out' and is the act of reducing or increasing the level of a sound over time. Fades can be automated within a digital audio workstation with different shapes of fading applied.

Fader   A control device found on a mixing-desk channel to alter the sound level of the signal passing through the channel.

Fat   A complimentary term applied to audio that has a big, warm, pleasant sound. The word is often associated with analogue sounds and the low end of the frequency spectrum and is often seen written in its alternative spelling of 'phat'.

Feedback   Occurs when an audio output is returned to the same audio input, thus creating a feedback loop. This can be heard by the accidental screech of a live PA system or by design as a guitarist controls the musical wailing of their guitar feedback.

Filter   A device that turns down or totally removes certain frequencies whilst passing other frequencies unaffected. The cut-off point for determining which frequencies are affected is set by the user. A high-pass filter will cut low frequencies, letting high frequencies pass, whilst a low-pass filter will cut high frequencies, letting low frequencies pass.

Flanger   A type of time-delay effect which also introduces a reoccurring phase-shift element.

Frequency   When relating to sound, frequency is the rate at which an object emitting sound vibrates. One vibration causes one sound wave. Measuring frequency is achieved by recording the number of sound waves per second. This measurement is returned in hertz or kilohertz (1,000 hertz = 1 kilohertz).

Frequency spectrum   Describes both the range of frequencies that a certain sound contains and the full scope of human hearing.

Gain   Refers to the loudness of audio, and in particular when loudness is increased or decreased.

A gain device is often the first device after an input and is used to regulate the incoming signal.

Gain reduction   The reduction of sound level. When a dynamics processor such as a compressor reduces the peaks of a passing signal it is said to reduce the gain or apply gain reduction.

Gain staging   A method of increasing or decreasing gain to ensure that each output passes the correct, expected level to the following input stage of an audio chain.

Gate   Or 'noise gate'. A sound processor that reduces the level of a signal below a user-set threshold. The threshold is the main setting by which the gate opens to let sound through or closes to reduce levels, although other controls are available to influence the response of the gate.

Glue   The effect certain mastering plugins have as they 'glue' instruments together to produce a good cohesive balance associated with professional mixes.

Hardware   Physical equipment that resides in the real world. Hardware can stand alone or be integrated into a computer where it interacts with software.

Harmonizer   A type of effect that duplicates a signal and then moves the copied sound both in pitch and in time to create new harmonies. The degree of movement in pitch and time can be subtle or drastic.

Harmony   Pleasing tones that are added to a melody to form more complex music.

HD   Or high definition. In audio terms, this is generally thought of as any audio with a specification that improves on the CD format (the format of CD being a sampling rate greater than 44.1kHz and a bit depth of more than 16 bits). High definition audio is usually referred to simply as HD audio.

Hertz   The unit of measurement for sound frequency, i.e. the number of sound waves per second. Hertz is abbreviated to Hz.

High end   Describes the highest frequencies within the frequency spectrum, which can also be referred to as 'top' or 'top end'.

High frequencies   The frequency spectrum can be divided into the three manageable bands named low, mid and high (each of which is often then subdivided for additional accuracy). High frequencies refers to the uppermost band.

High-pass filter   A device that reduces low frequencies whilst letting high frequencies pass unaltered (*see also* Filter).

Hold   A common control found within plugins that holds the current state of a device for a prede-termined time.

Import   To bring material into a project from an outside source. This may be a previously recorded instrument, a sample of a drum hit, a programmed MIDI part or a video clip, for example.

In-the-box   Describes the performance of audio-production tasks using a computer.

Input   The point at which audio enters a device. Inputs may be real inputs on physical hardware and instruments such as guitars, or virtual inputs on plugins, virtual instruments and a digital audio workstation's channels and busses.

Insert   To insert a plugin (or physical-effects unit) into a signal flow is to place the effect directly in the audio stream so that the whole of the signal is processed and no dry unprocessed signal remains. An insert point is a physical connection on a mixing desk that allows the engineer to route a signal through outboard hardware.

Kilohertz   A unit of measurement for sound frequency, i.e. the number of sound waves per second. One unit is equal to 1,000 hertz and can be abbreviated to kHz.

L-C-R   Stands for left, centre and right and refers to the three panning positions used in a style of mixing called L-C-R mixing.

Limiter   A type of dynamics processor that re-duces dynamic range in much the same way as a compressor does. In fact, traditional limiting is basically extreme compression. However, with the digital age came more advanced brick-wall limit-ers. It was this style of limiting that became an integral part of what we now refer to as the loud-ness war.

Limiting   The act of reducing dynamic range by the use of a limiter.

Loudness   The perceived level of sound. This is a subjective term that varies from person to person. One listener may think of a sound as being too loud while to another it may not appear loud enough!

Loudness war   Describes the battle that was fought over many years to produce the loudest masters. The driving factor was the notion that louder songs were perceived as better and would result in more sales. However, greater loudness led to degradation in quality as dynamics were squashed and audio became distorted and life-less.

Low end   Describes the lowest frequencies within the frequency spectrum.

Low frequencies   The frequency spectrum can be divided into three manageable bands known as low, mid and high (each of which is often then subdivided for additional accuracy). Low frequen-cies refers to the lowest band.

Low-pass filter   A device that reduces high frequencies whilst letting low frequencies pass unaltered (*see also* Filter).

Make-up   A control that increases gain (sound level) and is most often found on dynamics proc-essors, which work by reducing the loudest peaks of the audio signal. Make-up gain can then be applied to raise the signal back up to pre-proc-essed levels.

Master channel   Also referred to as the master buss or 'two buss', the master channel is the stereo channel on a mixing desk to which all other channels are routed.

Mastering   A term that has become blurred over recent times; mastering can be thought of as the final stage in audio production that takes a final mix, maximizes its impact and prepares it for the medium on which it will be replayed. Traditionally mastering has always been a separate process, but is becoming increasingly integrated into the mixing workflow.

Maximizer   A type of mastering brick-wall limiter that maximizes sound levels.

Melody   A sequence of single notes that forms the bare bones of a musical tune.

Meter   Within a musical context, 'meter' relates

to the expected number of bars and beats that a musical piece contains. 'Meter' is written at the start of a musical composition and at any point where the meter changes. Meter is expressed by two numbers, one above the other; the first number being the quantity of notes within each bar and the second being the length of note.

Microphone A device for recording analogue sound waves. The sound that is captured is converted into an electrical signal which can be recorded and processed or simply amplified for live music.

Mid frequencies The frequency spectrum can be divided into the three manageable bands known as low, mid and high (each of which is often then subdivided for additional accuracy). Mid frequencies refers to the middle of the three bands.

Mid range A term that is used to describe the middle frequencies within the frequency spectrum, often referred to simply as mid.

Mid/side Often written as M/S, this is first and foremost a recording technique for producing spatial stereo recordings. However, mid/side processing has become popular in recent years as more and more plugin developers add mid/side manipulation tools to their designs, giving the user independent control of the centre channel (mid) and the left and right channels (side).

MIDI Stands for Musical Instrument Digital Interface and is an all-encompassing technical Industry Standard for a communications protocol between digital musical devices, including all the processes and connections that are involved.

Milliseconds A measurement of passing time used in musical production. A millisecond is a subdivision of a second and is usually shortened to ms. There are one thousand milliseconds to a second.

Mix Can be the act of blending multi-track recordings into a stereo two-track format (or multi-channel surround sound). A mix engineer performs this mix. Alternatively, it may describe the actual article that is produced prior to the final mastering stage. A mix of a song is sent to a mastering engineer.

Mix engineer A specialist in the mixing stage of music production. It is a mix engineer's job to blend the multiple tracks of a live performance or recorded song and balance them in a professional manner in preparation for the final mastering stage.

Mixdown A mixdown is virtually the same as an export, and is, in fact, the act of exporting a mix to a stereo (or surround sound) format for use outside of the song's session. The purpose of this could be to pass the mix onto a mastering engineer or to provide review copies for production staff and artists. Whereas the term 'export' can be applied to any single track, 'mixdown' is only used when a complete mix is exported.

Mixing desk A device for accepting multiple sound sources and blending them via channels, busses and groups to a single stereo output (or surround-sound, multi-channel format).

Monitor Has multiple meanings regarding sound production. It could relate to a loudspeaker found in a recording studio; these are generally called monitors within pro-audio situations and speakers in consumer hi-fi-speak. Or it may mean the visual display unit that a digital audio workstation is viewed upon. When listening to a sound source whilst recording, you could also be said to be monitoring it.

Mono One channel played via one loudspeaker.

MP3 A coding format for digital audio that reduces the amount of data required to reproduce a song. Compression techniques are used to discard bits of data that have the least impact upon playback. When encoding audio to MP3 format, quality is sacrificed for convenience. But the benefits of a reduced file size mean that MP3 files can easily be transmitted by means that would be impossible without data compression.

Mud Describes the build-up of frequencies centered around 250Hz that 'muddies' a mix or a sound source.

Multi-effects A type of plugin (or hardware) that offers a chain of effects within one easily manageable box of tricks.

Multi-track Simply means multiple tracks are involved. For example, a multi-track recording is a recording that contains many separate tracks all time-aligned in perfect synchronization. A multi-track recorder is a device that is used to capture those multiple recordings.

Outboard   A collective name given to any hardware outside of a computer.

Output   The final connection within an audio device that passes the signal onto the input of the next unit in a chain. Every output is routed to the following input until the destination is an exported file or a loudspeaker. Outputs may be real or virtual and are found everywhere on channels, busses, groups, effects and processors.

Panning   To pan a sound source is to move it around the stereo sound-field using a device called a pan pot (an abbreviation of panning potentiometer). The pan pot is located on a mixing desk's channel strip. Panning is actually a form of level control. When sounds are moved to the left it is because the level feeding the right channel is being reduced. Likewise, moving sounds to the right is achieved by reducing the level of the left channel.

Parallel compression   A compression technique that mixes a second, compressed signal in with the original source. Parallel compression is also known as New York compression due to its origin.

Parametric equalizer   An equalizer that generally contains between two and six bands. It allows control over the width of the frequency range it is affecting, as well as the level. The control for width is known as Q. A parametric equalizer is also known as a peaking or bell-shaped equalizer.

Peak   The loudest momentary level of a sound or piece of music passing through electrical equipment.

Peak meter   A measurement tool for recording the peak level of a signal passing through audio equipment. A peak meter returns the peak value at any given time.

Phantom image   When audio is replayed via two speakers, a stereo sound-field is created and a phenomenon called the phantom image occurs. A phantom image happens when audio from the left speaker and the right speaker both contain identical sounds. Due to psychoacoustic laws,

the listening brain will place that particular sound centrally between the speakers.

Phase   In relation to music production, a phase can be thought of as the complete cycle of one sound wave. When two or more sound waves are combined, the sound waves can be said to be 'in phase' or 'out of phase', depending on the shape and timing of the individual waveforms.

Phase cancellation   When two sound waves are the exact opposite of each other, no sound will be audible as both waves cancel each other out due to a phenomenon known as phase cancellation. This is an example of total cancellation, but phase cancellation is happening all the time in varying degrees as multiple tracks fight against each other and produce patterns of phase cancellation at specific frequencies.

Phaser   An effect that takes a duplicate signal and filters notches in the sound wave, thus altering the shape of that wave. The altered sound is then modulated to create a sweeping effect as it is added back to the original signal.

Pitch   Musical pitch is the label given to each musical note to denote how high or low each note sounds. Musical pitch is generally written using a letter. C D E F G A B are the pitches that make up the C Major scale. However, every pitch also carries a unique frequency number. For example, the A above Middle C by which an orchestra tunes is 440Hz.

Pitch shift   To pitch shift a sound, or combination of sounds, is to move the pitch of the sound in question up or down. The degree of shifting can vary from tonal shifts (the pitches of a musical scale) to minute shifts that our ears cannot distinguish as pitches; for example, a shift in pitch of only a few cents is often used in certain types of effects plugins such as harmonizers.

Plugin   A collective name given to effects and processors that are 'plugged in' to the audio signal path. The name comes from the use of outboard effects units that were indeed physically plugged in to hardware mixing-desk channels.

Polarity   The state of having two opposite aspects. An electrical audio signal, therefore, has polarity (the two opposite aspects being the peak and dip of a sound wave). On a mixing-desk channel strip, polarity can be switched so that the peaks become dips and the dips become peaks. This is useful for aligning one sound wave with another and, therefore, reinforcing the sound.

Post-fader Describes anything that sits after a mixing-desk channel fader, for example, an auxiliary send or an audio processor.

Pre-delay A control generally found on a reverberation-effects unit. The pre-delay control adds an amount of time before which the effect is heard. This is useful to add perceived separation between the dry signal and the reverberation signal.

Pre-fader Describes anything that sits before a mixing-desk channel fader, for example, an auxiliary send or an audio processor.

Presence Describes how certain sounds appear more forward or present in the stereo field than others. To give a sound more presence, therefore, is to bring it out front in the mix. One way of achieving this is to boost a certain range of frequencies, which is why the range of frequencies in question is sometimes known as the presence range. These are centred around 4kHz or octave eight of the musical scale.

Processor Any plugin that processes the complete sound, i.e. when processing, the whole of the signal passes through a processor and no dry sound remains.

Psychoacoustics The area of science concerned with how human beings perceive and react to sound.

Q The control that varies the width of a frequency band within a parametric equalizer. The wider the Q, the more frequencies selected.

Range The number of frequencies that an individual equalizer band is affecting. Alternatively, a singer's vocal range is the range of notes they are able to sing comfortably.

Ratio A control found in dynamics processors such as compressors. The ratio setting varies the degree of dynamic-range reduction taking place; the higher the setting, the more compression. Ratio appears as two numbers, a before and after

compression figure, with each number representing a level of decibels in relationship to each other. For example, a ratio setting of 2:1 means a signal of 2db before compression will be reduced to 1db after compression.

Record Could mean to capture a sound or performance onto a recording medium such as a tape or hard disk. There is also a record button to achieve this. The word record is also used to describe an analogue vinyl disc, a sound-recording medium that is played on a record player.

Recording studio A building where sound recordings are captured. The term recording studio is generally applied to the large commercial studios, many of which have now closed down as musicians choose to record their own compositions in smaller 'project studios' at home.

Release The decay of a sound and the final portion of an 'attack, delay, sustain, release' or ADSR envelope found in sound design and synthesizers. Also, a release setting can be found on many effects units where it is used to smooth the transition of a signal that moves from being processed to unprocessed.

Render To render a record part, or a selection of many parts, is to export them to a new file. In many digital audio workstations the new rendered file will automatically replace the old ones. Rendering is useful for combining fragmented recordings into one easy-to-handle waveform or for freeing up processing power by rendering audio with active-effects plugins. The plugins can then be removed after rendering.

Reverberation Can be thought of as the prolonging of a sound within a given environment. Reverberation-effects units simulate a sound within a responsive environment, with many virtual environments to choose from.

Rhythm When playing or creating musical notes there are choices to make, and the decisions regarding how hard a note should be played and for how long determine the rhythm of a piece. Short and long notes mix with stressed and unstressed notes to form repeated patterns that we know as rhythm.

Roll off A term given to the reduction of frequencies. For example, to roll off the low end is to reduce low frequencies.

Routing The act of diverting a sound signal from one place to another. To send a signal from one channel to a buss, for example, is routing. All of the signal may be sent or a signal may be split to feed multiple destinations.

Routing grid Found within a digital audio workstation, a routing grid is a means of displaying, as an overview, the complete routing paths of all signals within a project.

Sample To sample can mean the act of sampling, e.g. the re-recording of a clip of music or a musical instrument for the purpose of playing back the sample via a sampler. Electronic musicians today often sample other artists' work. Alternatively, digital audio is also represented in samples, one sample being a digital snapshot of an analogue signal.

Sample rate The rate at which a digital device samples per second, a measurement that is expressed in kilohertz. For example, the compact disc format plays audio at 44,100 samples per second, or 44.1kHz.

Saturation *See* Tape saturation.

Semitone The smallest musical interval between two notes. To move a finger one step up or down the fret board of a guitar, or to play the next note up or down a piano keyboard is to move one semitone. Two semitones equal a tone.

Send and return loop When applied to the analogue world, a send and return loop is a form of routing. A signal is sent out of a mixing desk to be processed by outboard equipment and then returned back into the mixing desk via an unused channel or an auxiliary return. The same principle applies to virtual send and return loops found within a digital audio workstation.

Session The term given to a recording session. Back in the day, recording artists booked time slots in recording studios. These were called recording sessions. The word session has been carried forward to the digital audio workstation era with each new recording phase or project being labelled a session.

Shelf A shelf or shelving equalizer is a device that increases or decreases a range of frequencies equally below or above a certain point. A shelving equalizer will be either a high or low shelf as it affects only the highest and lowest areas of the frequency range.

Software Computer programs found within a computer. A digital audio workstation is a piece of software. Software interacts with hardware (the physical devices found outside of, or integrated into, a computer).

Sound engineer The person who is responsible for optimizing the quality of sounds at source during a studio recording session or live performance.

Sound-field The term given to the spatial illusion created by stereo sound recordings and productions within the stereo format.

Soundcard An audio interface that allows sounds from outside a computer to be processed digitally by the computer. A soundcard uses an analogue-to-digital converter to digitize analogue signals and a digital-to-analogue converter to return the signal back to the analogue world. Often a soundcard can accept signals in many formats and also pass on MIDI data.

Speaker Part of a hi-fi system found in domestic homes that is responsible for playing recorded sound and is also known as a loudspeaker.

Spectrum analyzer A sound production tool used to visually display the frequency content of a sound or mix of sounds.

SPL Stands for sound-pressure level and is the level of sound pressure measured in decibels.

SPL meter A device for measuring sound-pressure levels.

Stereo A format for reproducing sound recordings using two channels.

Submix The pre-mixing of individual sounds spread across multiple mixing-desk channels. The channels in question are balanced against each other and then routed to one new submix channel (two channels for stereo). The submix channel is then used as a controller. This is useful, for example, when mixing a drum kit. Many microphones can be used to record a drum kit; this can become unmanageable when trying to balance the drums against the rest of the mix. The answer is to submix them and control the level of all the drums with one fader.

Sustain   The third phase of an 'attack, decay, sustain, release' or ADSR envelope found in sound design and synthesizers. 'Sustain' can be used to describe any part of a sound that retains a certain level over a given time. To sustain a sound is to prolong its level.

Synesthesia   When related to music, synesthesia is a phenomenon that causes a listener to see different colours when hearing music. Specific frequencies or certain sounds trigger the colourful response.

Synthesizer   Often referred to simply as a synth, a synthesizer is an electrical musical instrument used to generate sound and can be analogue or digital.

Tape   An analogue sound-recording and archiving medium mostly reserved for prestige productions these days, having been superseded by cheaper, more user-friendly digital solutions.

Tape saturation   When using an analogue tape recorder to capture a sound source, it is possible to increase the input signal to a point where saturation of the tape is reached. Any further increase in the level past the saturation threshold will result in a squashed sound similar to compression. Recording sound to analogue tape is a creative process in itself and a skilled sound engineer will feed the perfect amount of signal to tape to achieve tape saturation if required. There are now many tape saturation plugins available in an attempt to bring analogue warmth to digital recording.

Template   A means of saving the complete set-up of a digital audio workstation; a template can then be recalled at a later date and used as a starting point for a new production, thus saving much time.

Tempo   The speed at which music is played. When relating to sound recording and mixing, tempo is represented by a beats-per-minute figure, which can be fixed for the duration of the song, increased or decreased at certain points along the timeline or disregarded altogether.

Threshold   A control used on audio processors to change the processing state from passive (not processing) to active (processing). A signal is dry when its level is below a threshold and wet as soon as it passes through the threshold level.

Timeline   The ruler-type display found in all digital audio workstations. The timeline starts at zero and counts upwards in time. All audio is placed along the timeline and time-stamped with a start and end time. A timeline can also display other means of counting passing events such as beats and bars, timecodes and video frames.

Tone   A control found on amplifiers and audio equipment that is used to alter the balance of frequency bands. Bass and treble controls are collectively called a tone control. Alternatively, the term 'tone' is also used by musicians such as guitarists who place a great deal of emphasis on perfecting their sound or tone.

Track   To track is to record a musical performance to a computer hard disk (or tape). Each performance is usually, but not always, recorded to a separate track within a digital audio workstation. The term 'track' remains from the days when recording to tape was the Industry Standard. A tape recorder was known by the number of tracks it was capable of recording, e.g. a 2-, 4- or 8-track recorder.

Transient   The very first spike of sound energy produced by a musical instrument. Transients contain a great deal of information that is used by our brains to recognize words or place sounds within an environment.

Transient designer   A device that enables the user to shape the response of a sound's transients *(see also* Transient).

Transparent audio   Describes audio that passes through a processing device unaltered.

Treble   Describes the upper frequency range of music, usually within consumer hi-fi speak.

Trim   Can be a name for a device that controls

sound level (*see also* Gain and Gain staging). Alternatively, to trim an audio waveform is to shorten a recorded clip in length.

Valve   A component found in analogue equipment that subjectively colours the passing sound in a musically pleasing way.

Vinyl   When relating to music, vinyl is a term given to an analogue sound-storage medium established many years ago. The vinyl record appeared to have gone out of fashion with the emergence of the compact disc and a certain death was predicted, but in recent times a new generation of music listeners has valued vinyl for its warm analogue sound and created a resurgence in the medium.

VU meter   VU stands for 'volume unit'. A VU meter is a tool for measuring the volume units (signal level) in audio equipment. A VU meter returns an averaged sound level over time, which is a more musical method than purely registering the peak value at any given time.

Warmth   A subjective term used to describe a certain quality of audio. Warmth is seen to be a good attribute and is generally used when referring to analogue signals. It is thought that warmth is a by-product of analogue components such as valves and the subtle distortion introduced by the analogue processes. Analogue warmth is often compared to digital coldness.

Wav   A shortened version of Waveform Audio File Format, which is probably the most common format for storing audio on computer. A 'wave' file is generally referred to as a 'wav' due to its file extension of .wav.

Waveform   The shape or form a sound wave takes when converted to an electrical signal, or when generated electronically. The term waveform can also be used to describe the visual representation of recorded audio in a digital audio workstation clip.

Wet   Describes a signal that has been, or is being, processed by any effects or processors.

Workflow   A modern word that encapsulates the whole process of music production from start to finish, but more often than not is applied to the various stages of digital in-the-box music production, e.g., tracking workflow, mixing workflow or mastering workflow.

INDEX

0dBFS   103
1176 peak limiter/compressor   47, 57–58
16 bit   68, 93, 96, 103, 105
24 bit   104–105
44.1kHz   68, 93, 96, 102–103
48kHz   103
acoustic guitar   46–47, 54
acoustic treatment   100–102
air   34–35, 37, 59, 88
analogue emulation   15, 41, 89–90, 102
Atkins, Rodney   7, 109–110
attack   95
Audio Technica   102
auto release   68, 95
auxiliary send and return   13, 42, 89
Avid   15, 102
B3 organ   51
back-up   69, 71
balance   78, 80, 85–86, 88, 94, 110
bass   46, 87
bass enhancer   45, 87
bass guitar   45–46, 78, 87–88
bit depth   68, 96, 103
boombox   85–86, 102
brightness   29, 54, 80, 88
buss   12, 39–43, 52–55, 62–65
buss compressor   68, 94–95
buss glue   68, 94
cents   54
channel   12, 25
channel strip   26, 29–32, 59, 62
chorus   80
Churko, Kevin   91
clip gain   73–74, 105
clipper   30, 41–42, 48
clipping   49, 95–96, 103–105
colour of sound   50, 68, 96
commercial CDs   81, 83, 85, 88–89, 94, 97, 102
compression   77, 84, 95
compressor   26, 29–32, 37, 40–42, 47, 57–59, 62,
    73, 80, 95

computer   9–11, 102
country music   45, 60, 89, 91, 110
dance music   19, 27
daw   11–12, 15, 17, 25, 42, 69
decay   68, 95
de-esser   59–60, 62–63, 89
delay   52–53, 63–64, 80
distortion   68, 103, 105
dither   34, 68, 96
double tracking   54, 89
doubler   53–54, 80
drums   17, 39–40, 42–43, 78
drum replacer   18–19, 21–22, 26–27, 31–35
dynamic range   57, 68, 78
dynamics   41, 68, 73, 78, 95
ear training   81–82
early reflections   54, 63
electric guitar   48–50
EQ matching   87, 97
equalizer   26, 28–32, 34–36, 38, 42, 45, 47–48,
    50–51, 59, 62, 78, 80–81, 94
equilateral triangle   101
Eventide H3000   54, 64
export   71, 96, 104
fader   40, 78
fader riding   13, 35, 57–58, 84
filter   26, 29
flanger   53, 80
frequency spectrum   67, 81–82, 94
frequency analyzer   87–88, 97
gain reduction   57, 67, 95–96
gain staging   41, 57, 69, 73–75, 80
gate   32
guitar amp simulator   45
hardware   54, 85–86
headroom   67, 103
hertz   82, 102
high pass filter   26, 29–30, 32, 34, 36, 41, 45–47,
    59, 62, 67, 87
hi-hat   17, 34
import   71–73

insert   13, 15
in-the-box   54, 90, 102, 107
kick drum   17–20, 25–27, 73, 87–88
kilohertz   82, 102
level matching   81
limiter   41, 73, 80, 84, 96
limiter/maximizer   34, 39, 47, 49–51, 68, 75, 94–96
Lord-Alge, Chris   68, 90–91
loudness war   96–97
low pass filter   29–32, 47, 67
low-end   20, 45–46 54, 59, 87
low-mid   27, 35
Mackie HR824 Mk2   85
make-up gain   37
masking   78–79, 81
master channel   12, 17, 43, 67–68, 74–75, 77, 87, 95, 103
mastering   10, 69, 93–97
mastering engineer   68, 102
memory man   53
metal music   45, 110
metering   97
microphone   88, 99
mid/side   87
mixing   14, 68, 77–91, 93, 97, 100
mixing desk   15, 77, 85, 100
monitor gain   85
monitors   85–86, 100–102
mono   15, 62, 80, 84, 86
mud   47, 59, 87–88
multi-effects   59, 62, 68, 94–95
music   9, 77, 90–91, 96, 99
mute   78
Nashville   14, 17, 89, 91, 93, 101, 109
null test   60
octave   82
outboard   54
overhead microphone   17, 36–37
panning   37, 54, 80–81, 84–86
parallel compression   17, 39–40, 42, 80, 90, 95
percussion   39, 73
Peterzell, Lynn   91
phantom image   80, 85
phase cancellation   40, 60–61, 100
phaser   53–54, 64
piano   51
pitch shifting   54
plugin   13–15, 59, 69, 74, 77, 87, 89, 94, 103
polarity   60–61, 89
pop music   60
post-fader   13, 69
pre-delay   54, 86

pre-fader   13, 63, 69
pre-master-channel control fader   69
presence   29–30, 41, 47–48
presets   53
pro tools   12, 89, 102
psychoacoustics   46, 79, 88
Q   59
Quested 18 subwoofer   85
ratio   40–41, 47, 68, 77, 95
recording studio   100
reference mixing   86, 89, 94
reverberation   17–23, 33–34, 37, 53–54, 62–63, 80, 90
reverse cymbal   28
rock music   45, 60, 68, 95–96
room   17, 37, 54, 85, 100
routing grid   43, 55, 65
sample rate   72, 102
samples   17–23, 37, 40, 73
semitone   54
Shipley, Mike   91
sibilance   60
snare drum   17–21, 29–34, 42, 73, 87, 90
spectrum analyzer   81, 83
spl meter   85
SSL   102
Staub, Randy   91
steel guitar   50, 85
stereo   15, 62, 67, 79–81, 84, 86
stereo widening   80
streaming   96
submix   23, 39–40
summing   60
synesthesia   82–83
synthesizer   51–52
tambourine   39
tape saturation   41, 95
template   9, 10–12, 17, 40, 69, 88, 94, 110
tempo   53, 72
time   53, 80
tom tom   17–18, 21–23, 35–36
total recall   11, 90
track   12, 71
transient designer   33
transients   30, 41, 48, 73
transparent   48, 50, 68, 96
vocal   9, 54, 80, 88–89
    background   57, 61–62, 64
    lead   54, 57, 83, 88
Wathen Reference .5   85
waveform   49, 61, 72, 78
weight   29, 35
workflow   10, 78